✳ TABLE OF CONTENTS

"If you hang out with her, we are so not friends anymore."

"Don't let Shannon sit at our table today."

"Don't talk to her."

"Hey, check out what Cheryl put on the website about Allison – it's a riot!"

"Your outfits ugly... just kidding!"

Eye rolls..., back turns..., whispers..., gossips...

Fear, Insecurity, Control, Power — all motivators of behavior in the girl world.

Don't ignore it – don't just say it's what girls do… it has been taken to new lengths with cell phones – text messaging, internet – IMing. It is doing more damage than ever before… damage to the person's develop of a worthwhile productive person… damage to a person who is getting reinforced for using hurtful ways to get what they want… damage to the adults they are becoming. We need to become more aware of the hidden ways that girls bully one another. We need to give support and empower the victim, to encourage the bystander to take a stand, and to guide the aggressor to find appropriate ways to meet her needs.

Let's take a closer look at the

WHAT?

WHY?

and HOW?

to help girl bullying...

What Is Girl Bullying?

Bullying is repeated behavior intended to harm or hurt someone physically, emotionally, or socially and typically involves an imbalance or a perceived imbalance of power.

Girl bullying can take on the form of either Direct Bullying or Indirect Bullying. **Direct Bullying** is more open and aggressive such as shoving, pushing, threatening, "in your face" type bullying and the **Indirect Bullying** is more hidden, "behind your back" type of bullying that includes such behaviors as exclusions, hurtful teasing, gossips, rumors, bossing, controlling, manipulation, and intimidation. Girls can display both direct and indirect bullying, however the indirect bullying is more typical of girls.

As we further explore girl bullying and the forces that motivate the bullying, it brings us to attempting to understand the complicated Girls' World. Girls are typically more social oriented beings who form their identities from relationships with others. Girls value the importance of fitting in and having friends. A girl's friendships can provide closeness, comfort, and fun, but can also be the source of the most pain and hurt. In attempts to survive the girls' world they can resort to spreading rumors, gossips, hurtful teasing, controlling, manipulating, betraying a friend, and more – girl bullying.

Some of the typical roles within the girls' social group are:[*]

❋ The leader or the **"Queen"** is the one who has the power of the group and can resort to manipulation and control to keep the power.

❋ The **"Sidekick"** is the person who always supports the queen because that is where the power is, she allows herself to be controlled and manipulated, in order to fit in.

[*] Information is adapted with permission from the MEAN GIRLS professional seminar provided by Developmental Resources, Inc. (1-800-251-6805).

✳ The **"Wannabee"** is the person who wants to be just like the leader enjoying the power/popularity and will go to great lengths to get the approval.

✳ The **"Gossiper"** gains her power from seeking information from others to improve her position.

✳ The **"Floater"** is the girl who moves in and out of different groups not needing a specific group for her self-esteem and identity. She does not seek power but shows respect and does not exclude other girls.

✳ The **"Direct Bully"** is the girl who uses physical violence with pushing, shoving, and threatening types of behavior.

✳ The **"Target"** is the person receiving the hurtful, mean behaviors. She can become a victim when she allows the other girls' indirect bullying and mean behaviors of exclusion, rumors, eye-rolls, hurtful teasing, etc. to negatively affect herself by feeling humiliated, exposed, and tempted to change to fit in.

✳ The **"Bystander"** is the person who witnesses the bullying or mean girl behavior and can feel caught in the middle. She may be afraid of being the next victim or afraid to go against the one with the power or not wanting to choose sides between friends.

Caution is given to using these labels in speaking to or in referencing the girls or their friends. Information is given more so for understanding of how complicated the girls' world can be in trying to maneuver within their social relationships.

A term coined by Dr. Nicki Crick in the early nineties - Relational Aggression or "RA" - seems to describe the type of bullying found in the girls' world. **Relational aggression** uses aggressive or hurtful behavior to harm someone by damaging or manipulating his or her relationships with others. The purpose of relational aggression is to socially exclude or damage a person's reputation or status within the peer group and can be motivated by either fear of not being a part of a group or to gain power and prestige in a desired group.

Within the bullying situation three roles emerge – the aggressor or the bully, the target/victim, and the bystander. The three roles can be further explained as:

❏ The one doing the aggressing–the aggressor or **Bully Behavior**. The term "bully behavior" is used rather than "bully" as we focus on separating the behavior from the person (the person is not 'bad' but their choice to use hurtful or mean behaviors is 'bad'). It is important here to realize that when we talk of "bully behaviors" we are including not just the direct bullying of hitting, pushing, shoving, threatening, but also the indirect forms of bullying that include exclusion, gossiping, spreading rumors, bossing, controlling, intimidating, hurtful teasing, manipulation.

❏ The **Target or Victim** is the person being bullied. A person can be a target without being a victim by choosing not to let the bully behavior affect her in a negative way.

❏ The **Bystander** is the witness or person standing by seeing the problem. Bystanders have the power to make a positive difference in the situation.

As we apply these three roles to girl bullying or relational aggression, we need to realize that girls typically end up in each role at some point – either participating in the mean or bullying behavior or being a target or victim of that behavior and at times caught in the middle. Girls can easily move in and out of each of these three roles. To understand this we look to the motivating factors for each of these roles.

The girl bullying/relational aggressive behavior appears to be motivated by underlying fear and insecurity. The aggressor may be insecure and worried about remaining "on top" so she uses manipulation and control of others to avoid having her own weaknesses exposed. The victim often lacks the confidence to stand up for herself and may feel that she deserves the ill treatment. The bystander is afraid and lacks the self-confidence to take a stand and may join in the aggression, either passively or overtly, to avoid being targeted themselves. **By understanding the underlying factors, this gives us insight as to strategies and skill building that are needed to counteract the relational aggression or girl bullying.** The first step to counteracting girl bullying is an awareness of the hidden girl bullying. Awareness can encourage and empower people to want to make a difference. The second step is gaining an understanding that these are behaviors we don't have to accept. And the third step is sharing support and skill building for dealing with and/or reducing girl bullying behavior.

Why is it important to address this problem?

Loneliness, depression, self-injury, poor academic performance, low self-esteem, suicide ideation, anger. A girl who is repeatedly victimized by others may come to accept this treatment as normal and stay in unhealthy relationships later in life. It's important to break the cycle now.

The preteen and teen years are so important because girls search for their identity, beliefs about themselves – who they are and who they will become – and form beliefs about others and how to interact. **Our goal is to help our young girls become self assured, independent, confident adults who interact with others in a healthy, helping way.** We do not want to ignore the problem, we do not want our young girls carrying a negative perception into adulthood - either battling low self-worth as they function in their adult relationships and jobs or by choosing manipulation and control to gain their power.

Research on Relational Aggression fromDellasega and Nixon's book *Girl Wars* states that:

✻ Relationally aggressive behavior is evident in all age groups from preschool through adulthood.

✻ For students in grades three through six, relational aggression is a stronger predictor of future social maladjustment than overt physical aggression.

✻ Relational aggression is connected to peer rejection, decreased acts of pro-social behavior, and antisocial and borderline personality features in young adults.

✻ Both victims and initiators of relational aggression have a higher incidence of serious mental health problems such as depression, loneliness, alienation, emotional distress, and isolation.

✻ Studies show that relational aggression is linked to physical violence.

According to the National Association of School Psychologists (NASP), approximately one in seven school children is a bully or a victim, and the problem directly affects about five million elementary and junior high students in the United States. For fourth through eight graders, 22 percent report academic difficulties resulting from peer abuse.

So... how do we help?
Read on...

How do you address the problem of girl bullying?

The FIRST STEP is an awareness of the girl bullying (relational aggression) – what it looks like and how it can negatively impact:

❋ Awareness is important for the administration in the school in order to gain their support and backing for school-wide initiatives.

❋ Awareness is important for teachers since they are on the front line in dealing with the girls and can utilize strategies to prevent and intervene in helpful ways.

❋ Awareness is important for parents so they can understand and provide support for their daughters.

❋ Awareness is important for the students so they can actually label and understand what is going on. To empower them to make a difference, to change for the positive in whatever role they are playing: the aggressor, the target, or the bystander.

❋ Awareness is important for counselors of girl bullying so that helpful skills can be included in classroom lessons, small groups, and individual counseling to address the problem of girl bullying.

An awareness of girl bullying brings us to the SECOND STEP, which is the desire to change and make a difference. This desire encourages action from all involved, either through support, skill development, empowerment, education, or redirection.

The THIRD STEP involves providing the specific strategies and skills needed for reducing girl bullying and its' harmful affects.

The following Chapters of this book provide strategies for each of these steps - for the awareness of the hidden forms of girl bullying, for the motivation and desire to change, and for implementing the specific skills and strategies to help in dealing with girl bullying:

CHAPTER 1: SCHOOL-WIDE APPROACH to BULLYING

✳ Provides research information and handouts that can be shared with administration on how girl bullying not only negatively impacts the individual but negatively impacts the learning environment.

✳ Provides information to create overheads or power point presentation for a teacher in-service on bullying which emphasizes an understanding of girl bullying. The goal of the in-service is to promote awareness and action in dealing with the problem of bullying. Slides and notes are included in this section to guide the discussion and learning for teachers.

✳ Provides a school survey to utilize with students to gain a better understanding of the reality of what your students are experiencing.

✳ Provides suggestions, strategies, and activities for teachers in supporting, preventing, and dealing with the problem of girl bullying.

✳ Provides suggestions for school-wide approaches.

CHAPTER 2: CLASS LESSONS ON BULLYING

✳ Provides information to create overheads or a power point presentation for a class lesson on the topic of bullying entitled, **Bullying: What's It All About?** Information on bullying, examples and differences between girl and boy bullying, as well as strategies to help, are given. Through examples, an emphasis is placed on including the hurtful behaviors of relational aggression as bullying behaviors. Only when we recognize and admit the behavior is not acceptable can we then work to make a change.

✳ Other class lessons in this chapter address the three roles of bullying and include:

❑ **What's in Your Heart?** – focus is on reviewing their own behavior and making changes to be more kind and caring to others.

❑ **Bully Proof Defense Shield** – focus is on learning strategies for handling the situation when you are the target of bullying.

❑ **Bystander** – focus is on reviewing how the bystander can help in a bully situation.

CHAPTER 3: PARENT INFORMATION ON GIRL BULLYING

- Provides information to create overheads or power point presentation for a parent workshop on girl bullying. The goal of the workshop is to promote awareness and action for parents in supporting their daughters in understanding the girls' world and for dealing with the problem of relational aggression or girl bullying that is a part of their world.
- Handouts and guidelines for suggestions and strategies to share with parents are given in this section.
- Suggestions for resources for a Parent Book Club are also given.

CHAPTER 4: SMALL GROUP COUNSELING SESSIONS on GIRL BULLYING

- Information is given on Small Group Counseling on the topic of "Girl Bullying". This section includes a needs assessment, creative small group activities for discussion and learning, and a post assessment. See Chapter four for a list of the ten lessons.

CHAPTER 5: INDIVIDUAL COUNSELING ACTIVITIES on GIRL BULLYING

- Provides strategies for supporting and counseling girls dealing with the issue of girl bullying. Counseling activities are included to address both the needs of the aggressor and the victim. See Chapter six for a listing of specific activities.

School-Wide Approach to Bullying

A basic understanding and implementation of a School-wide Bully Prevention Program is essential. The definition of bullying is: repeated behaviors intended to harm or hurt someone physically, emotionally, or socially and typically involves an imbalance or perceived imbalance of power. The definition of relational aggression is: behavior that is intended to harm someone by damaging or manipulating the relationships with others. Relational Aggression is the predominant form of bullying used by girls. Relational Aggression uses the complicated structure of the girls' world to achieve power and security at others' expense. **Due to the rise in relational aggression (girl bullying) and the negative long lasting effects, it warrants our understanding and focused efforts to make a difference**. In order to address girl bullying in a school setting of both males and females this information will follow the structure of a Bully Prevention Program with emphasis on understanding the significance of girl bullying in terms of relational aggression. This Chapter will provide information that includes and focuses on Girl Bullying that can be used as part of your established bully prevention program OR the lessons and teacher in-service can be the framework for your Bully Prevention Program. The material in this book operates under the following premises.

There are three roles of Bullying:

✳ **Aggressor or Bully Behavior** – (The term Bully Behavior is used to avoid the negative connotation and the preconceived notions when using the word "bully".) Both Direct Bullying of hitting, pushing, shoving, threatening are explored, as well as, Indirect Bullying of exclusion, spreading rumors, gossiping, hurtful teasing, bossing, controlling, and manipulating. Girls typically bully through relational aggression; therefore, relational aggression examples are emphasized as situations from the girls world are shared to help others recognize that intentional hurting within relationships is also bullying and is not okay.

✳ **Target/Victim** – A person can be a target without being a victim by choosing not to let the bully behavior affect them in a negative way.

✳ **Bystander** – The bystander is the witness or person standing by seeing the problem. Bystanders have the power to make a positive difference in the situation.

People can frequently move in and out of these three roles. Strategies and options for prevention and intervention need to be taught to the students and reinforced so that:
- the student can be more aware of their negative behaviors to change,
- when a student is a target they can prevent themselves from becoming a victim of bullying,
- bystanders are encouraged to get actively involved in helping others.

The Bully Prevention Program needs to be a school-wide approach including administration involvement, faculty in-service, parent information, and student information and skill building.

The success of any school program lies within the support of the administration. When the administration believes in the value of the program in the educational setting then he/she can provide time and encouragement for school-emphasis focusing on teacher training and involvement, parent workshops, information and support for students through class lessons, small group counseling, and individual counseling. Therefore, this chapter begins with a **HANDOUT FOR ADMINISTRATORS** that includes a rational and statistics that are intended to facilitate a dialogue with administrators focused on the need to address the issue of bullying, including an emphasis on girl bullying (relational aggression).

This chapter includes a **SCHOOL SURVEY ON BULLYING** that includes girl bullying - relationally aggressive behaviors. The survey can be used as a pre assessment in order to target the specific needs of the class, grade, or school and to target the needed areas of increased supervision. After program implementation, the School Survey on Bullying can be used again as a post assessment tool.

This chapter includes a **TEACHER IN-SERVICE** and **TEACHER HANDOUT** for an awareness of the need to address the problems of bullying, including: the harmful effects of relational aggression, an understanding of the roles of bullying, how girls may bully differently than boys, and effective strategies for helping our students in each of the three roles.

TEACHER-LED CLASS ACTIVITIES are given in this chapter so that teachers have a concrete, brief activity to use that can:

- open up discussions and dialogue for students on bullying,

- bring awareness of all types of bullying and recognition of behaviors intended to hurt or harm that are not okay,

- allow students the opportunity to personalize what they might do in a difficult situation, encourage, value, and appreciate caring behavior.

The class activities allow a quick, easy way to extend the learning.

The chapter also includes **SCHOOL-WIDE ACTIVITIES** such as assemblies, mix-it up day, poster contest, commercials during announcements, and wall displays so that the awareness of bullying is continually brought to people's attentions so that together we can make a difference.

THE NEED FOR ADDRESSING GIRL BULLYING FROM WITHIN THE BULLY PREVENTION PROGRAM: STATISTICS AND RATIONALE

WHAT?

■ Bullying is a pattern of repeated behavior (physical, verbal, emotional) that is intended to hurt someone else. Usually involves an imbalance of power.

■ Girls typically bully different from boys. Girls form their identity within their social relationships. It is within their friendship groups that girl bullying (relational aggression) can be extremely harmful. Motivated by insecurity and fear and seeking to gain power, girls can start rumors, spread gossip, tease, exclude, manipulate, control, etc. Physical bullying can hurt the outside of the body, but emotional/social bullying can hurt the body from the inside and do more damage.

WHY?

■ According to the National Association of School Psychologists (NASP), approximately one in seven school children is a bully or a victim, and the problem directly affects about five million elementary and junior high students in the United States. For fourth through eighth graders, 22 percent report academic difficulties resulting from peer abuse.

■ Child bullies are at a greater risk for problems in the future. For example, by age thirty, 25 percent of the adults who had been identified as bullies as children had a criminal record, as opposed to 5 percent of the adults who hadn't been bullies (*Bullies and Victims* by SuEllen Fried and Paula Fried. New York: M. Evans and Company, 1994).

■ 25% of students report that teachers intervene in bullying situations, while 71% of teachers believe they always intervene. (www.bullybeware.com) . Bullying can be covert and executed underneath the adults radar.

■ Many states have legislation mandating bully prevention programs in schools – is yours one?

■ Using social relationships to harm others, was coined by researcher Nicki Crick from the University of Minnesota as Relational Aggression (RA) and is often associated with girl bullying.

- Information and research on RA from *Girl Wars* by Cheryl Dellasega and C. Nixon shows that:

  ❑ RA is evident in all age groups from preschool through adulthood

  ❑ For students in Grades 3-6, relational aggression is a stronger predictor of future social maladjustment than overt physical aggression.

  ❑ Both victims and initiators of RA have a higher incidence of serious mental health problems such as depression, loneliness, alienation, emotional distress, and isolation.

  ❑ Children of today are rehearsing their adult roles of tomorrow. Do we want adults using rumors and manipulation to gain power? Do we want adults that because they were victimized as children, think it's okay to be victimized as an adult?

HOW?

- Implement a School-Wide Bully Prevention Program which includes an emphasis on Girl Bullying and Relational Aggression. School-wide program may include:

  ❑ Bully survey to gather information.

  ❑ Establish clear school-wide and classroom rules about bullying including relational aggression.

  ❑ Provide an awareness and information for teachers on bullying (all forms including girl bullying) and encourage their sensitivity and consistency in dealing with bullying problems.

  ❑ Provide lessons and information to students for awareness and for skill development for prevention of bullying problems

  ❑ Provide support and skill development for students involved in bullying situations.

Date of Survey: _____

STUDENT SURVEY on SCHOOL BULLYING

Age: _____ Grade: _____   Check One: ☐ Male ☐ Female

Definition of Bullying: Bullying is repeated behavior that is meant to harm or hurt someone physically, emotionally, or socially and usually involves an imbalance of power.

Directions: Read each question and answer honestly.

	NEVER	SOMETIMES *Several times per month*	OFTEN *Several times per week*
1. I have been bullied by being hit, pushed, or kicked.	☐	☐	☐
2. I have been called names.	☐	☐	☐
3. I have been teased.	☐	☐	☐
4. I have been threatened or intimidated by others.	☐	☐	☐
5. I have been excluded or left out on purpose.	☐	☐	☐
6. I have had rumors spread about me.	☐	☐	☐
7. I have been talked about on the internet or phone in a hurtful way.	☐	☐	☐
8. I have had eyes rolled at me in a mean way.	☐	☐	☐
9. Other: _____	☐	☐	☐

	NEVER	SOMETIMES *Several times per month*	OFTEN *Several times per week*
10. I have bullied others by hitting, pushing or kicking.	☐	☐	☐
11. I have called others names.	☐	☐	☐
12. I have teased others.	☐	☐	☐
13. I have threatened or intimidated others.	☐	☐	☐
14. I have excluded or left out someone on purpose.	☐	☐	☐
15. I have spread mean rumors about someone.	☐	☐	☐
16. I have talked about others in a hurtful way on the internet or phone.	☐	☐	☐
17. Other: _____	☐	☐	☐

SCHOOL-WIDE APPROACH TO BULLYING

REPRODUCIBLE SURVEY

If you have been bullied by others this school year answer questions 18-20.
If not skip ahead to # 21.

18. Put a check mark by the place(s) you are usually bullied:
- ☐ school bus
- ☐ classroom
- ☐ recess
- ☐ lunchroom
- ☐ restroom
- ☐ on the internet or phone
- ☐ school hallways
- ☐ Other _____

19. Put a check mark by the students who usually bully you:
- ☐ boys   ☐ girls   ☐ group

Put a check mark by the age of the students who usually bother you:
- ☐ someone younger   ☐ someone older   ☐ same age

20. Did you tell someone about the bullying?
- ☐ Yes   ☐ No
(If yes, check all that apply)

- ☐ friend
- ☐ parent
- ☐ adult at school
- ☐ brother or sister
- ☐ Other: _____

If YES, do you feel they handled it well? ☐ Yes   ☐ No   ☐ Not Sure

21. Do you think our school handles bullying well? ☐ Yes   ☐ No   ☐ Not Sure

22. Do you feel safe from bullies at our school? ☐ Yes   ☐ No   ☐ Not Sure

Comments: _____

_____

_____

TEACHER IN-SERVICE ON STUDENT BULLYING

Purpose:

For the success of any program it is important to gain the commitment of the teachers, who are on the front lines with the students. The goals for the teacher in-service are:

* to identify what bullying is and what it looks like,
* to understand the problem and its negative immediate effects and future negative effects,
* to give a common language for everyone in the school – teachers, administrators, staff, students, and parents – in dealing with bullying,
* to empower the teachers so that he/she can make a difference,
* to give the teacher the tools/strategies to make that difference for the students.

Materials Needed:

* Copy overhead transparencies of pages 22-33 or create a Power Point presentation using the information given.
* Information folder created for each teacher. The following information needs to be copied and included in each folder – the sheet will be referred to in the In-Service:
  ✔ Classroom summary poster, "The Roles of Bullying and What to Do" on page 34. Provide a copy for the teachers so they will have the summary information and can direct the student to helpful information on the sheet.
  ✔ Bully Behavior Reporting Form page 35.
  ✔ Behavior Change Worksheet page 93.
  ✔ Review the **CLASS ACTIVITIES ON BULLYING** on pages 36-51 to determine which reproducible teacher-led activities meet the needs of your school. Copy these activities and add to each folder.

Procedure:

* Show the slide information and discuss. Use the **DISCUSSION INFORMATION** given at the bottom of each page as a guideline to guide and facilitate the discussion.

* Information regarding the bullying program that is shared in this in-service is based on the bullying information that is presented to students in the introductory class lesson, "Bullying: What's It All About?" located in the **CLASS LESSONS** Chapter of this book. If your school has a different emphasis please make changes or include your information.

WHAT IS BULLYING?

WHAT ARE SOME EXAMPLES OF BULLYING BEHAVIOR?

Welcome the teachers.

Hand out the teacher folders with the pre-selected, copied information. Several sheets will be referenced during the presentation.

DISCUSSION INFORMATION:

Encourage teachers to talk giving examples of bullying. Share that one definition of Bullying is a pattern of repeated mean behavior that is intended to harm physically, emotionally, or socially and usually has an imbalance of power.

Adults and students typically begin with bullying examples such as physical – hits, pushes, "fist in your face" or threats to others. If it is not shared ask if the following are examples of bullying: exclusion, rumors, eye-rolling, name-calling, teasing, spreading mean words about someone by note, computer email, text message, etc. Emphasize to the teacher that these too are bullying behaviors.

HOW DO GIRLS TYPICALLY BULLY DIFFERENTLY THAN BOYS?

DISCUSSION INFORMATION:

As teachers share, emphasize the following about the differences:

- *Boys typically use methods such as hitting, fighting, and threatening. These "face to face" methods, or direct bullying, are often more easy to observe.*

- *Girls often use the "behind the back" or indirect form of bullying which is harder to see. The indirect bullying behaviors include more subtle behaviors such as getting peers to exclude others and spreading rumors and gossip. The main purpose of the indirect bullying is typically social exclusion or damaging a person's reputation or status within the peer group. Relational problems demand more attention due to the complexity and are more time consuming and harder to deal with.*

- *Share that it is important to remember that BOTH girls and boys can use BOTH direct and indirect bullying methods.*

UNDERSTANDING THE GIRLS' WORLD

- **Girls are typically social beings with their identity gained within social groups.**

- **Relational Aggression is:**
  - **Aggressive, hurtful behaviors from within social relationships or friendship groups**

  - **Main form of bullying used by girls (Girl Bullying)**

DISCUSSION INFORMATION:

- *Girls are typically more social oriented beings who form their identities from relationships with others. Girls value the importance of fitting in and having friends. A girl's friendships can provide closeness, comfort, and fun, but can also be the source of the most pain and hurt. In attempts to survive in the girls' world they can resort to spreading rumors, gossip, hurtful teasing, controlling, manipulating, betraying a friend, and more – girl bullying.*

- *Relational aggression or "RA" is a term coined by Dr. Nicki Crick in the early nineties and involves aggressive or hurtful behavior that is exhibited within a social relationship. The purpose of these indirect bullying behaviors is to socially exclude or damage a person's reputation or status within the peer group and can be motivated by either fear of not being a part of a group or to gain power and prestige in a desired group. The main form of girl bullying is the more covert, hidden relational aggression; however girls can also bully openly, with aggressive, direct behavior of pushing, shoving, threatening, etc.*

THE ROLES WITHIN THE GIRLS' SOCIAL GROUP*

**The Queen
The Sidekick
The Wannabee
The Gossiper
The Floater
The Direct Bully
The Target
The Bystander**

Information adapted with permission from the MEAN GIRLS professional seminar provided by Developmental Resources, Inc.

DISCUSSION INFORMATION:

Briefly explore some of the possible roles within a friendship group:

- The leader or the " Queen" is the one who has the power of the group and can resort to manipulation and control to keep the power.
- The "Sidekick" is the person who always supports the queen because that is where the power is, she allows herself to be controlled and manipulated in order to fit in.
- The "Wannabee" is the person who wants to be just like the leader enjoying the power/popularity and will go to great lengths to get the approval.
- The "Gossiper" gains her power from seeking information from others to improve her position.
- The "Floater" is the girl who moves in and out of different groups not needing a specific group for her self-esteem and identity. She does not seek power but shows respect and does not exclude other girls.
- The "Direct Bully" is the girl who uses physical violence with pushing, shoving, and threatening types of behavior.
- The "Target" is the person receiving the hurtful, mean behaviors. She can become a victim when she allows the other girls' indirect bullying and mean behaviors of exclusion, rumors, eye-rolls, hurtful teasing, etc. to negatively affect herself by feeling humiliated, exposed, and tempted to change to fit in.
- The "Bystander" is the person who witnesses the bullying or mean girl behavior and can feel caught in the middle. She may be afraid of being the next victim or to go against the one with the power or she may not want to choose sides between friends.

Caution the teacher against using these labels in speaking to or in referencing/labeling students. Information is given for understanding of how complicated the girls' world can be in trying to maneuver within their social relationships.

WHY ADDRESS BULLYING IN SCHOOLS?

- **Negative/harmful affects**

- **Lower level bullying escalates in later years**

- **Statistics**

- **Role rehearsal for adulthood**

- **Significant incident and the police ask – what prevention programs were in place?**

- **New legislation**

- **Because we CARE...**

DISCUSSION INFORMATION:

- *Share the following negative effects: loneliness, depression, self-injury, poor academic performance, low self-esteem, suicide ideation, anger. All of which distract from the learning process.*
- *Point out that the problem of bullying, if ignored, will only get worse. Let's address this problem as early as possible to make a difference.*
- *According to the National Association of School Psychologists (NASP), approximately one in seven school children is a bully or a victim. For fourth through eighth graders, 22 percent report academic difficulties resulting from peer abuse. By age thirty, 25 percent of the adults who had been identified as bullies as children had a criminal record, as opposed to 5 percent of the adults who hadn't been bullies (Bullies and Victims by SuEllen Fried and Paula Fried. New York: M. Evans and Company, 1994). 25% of students report that teachers intervene in bullying situations, while 71% of teachers believe they always intervene. (www.bullybeware.com). Bullying can be covert and executed underneath the adults' radar.*
- *Students use their relationships with others to rehearse their roles for adulthood. What kind of adults do we want?*
- *Don't wait for something significant to happen before we put a helping plan/program into action.*
- *(Include only if your state mandates a school-wide program on bullying. If so, share that the law requires that bullying be addressed)*
- *Most of all, we address the issue of bullying, because we care.*

ALL – TEACHERS, STAFF, ADMINISTRATORS, PARENTS, STUDENTS NEED TO "SPEAK THE SAME LANGUAGE" IN REGARDS TO BULLYING IN ORDER TO ADDRESS THIS PROBLEM.

The main points shared in our introductory class lesson for students are:

1. **Bullying is defined as:** repeated behaviors intended to hurt someone physically, emotionally, or socially and involves an imbalance of power

2. **Three roles of bullying: Aggressor (Bully Behavior), Target/Victim, Bystander**

3. **IN/OUT Rule***

4. **Difference between a Conflict and Bullying.**

Concept used with permission from <u>No Room For Bullies</u> (2005). Boys Town Press, Boys Town: Nebraska.

DISCUSSION INFORMATION, SHARE THE FOLLOWING:

1. *Help to understand that bullying is repeated behaviors with intention to harm usually with an imbalance of power: physically or socially. Explain that the social imbalance of power is either a person that is "perceived" as being more popular or who has the skill level to "out talk" the other person. Bullying includes relational aggression.*

2. *Emphasize that the BULLY BEHAVIOR includes both physical, social, and emotional. Explain that the person who is the TARGET/VICITM is the person receiving the bullying behavior but that a person can be a target without being a victim by choosing not to let the bully behavior affect them in a negative way. Share that the BYSTANDER is the person standing by who witnesses the bullying. Explain that a bystander may feel scared that they'll be the next target, or they are so use to bullying behavior that they ignore it, or the bystander may laugh or join in with the bullying. Share that none of these approaches are helpful. The bystander has the power to make a difference by getting involved to help.*

3. *Explain that the IN/OUT Rule helps differentiate between tattling and telling. If you are trying to get someone OUT of trouble then tell; however if you are trying to get someone IN trouble then it's tattling – don't.*

4. *A conflict is a disagreement of equal powers; Bullying has the intent to hurt and has an imbalance of power. Conflicts are a normal part of life, bullying is not.*

WHAT CAN
WE DO
TO HELP?

Support the student in each of the 3 roles:

- **BULLY BEHAVIOR**

- **TARGET/VICTIM**

- **BYSTANDER**

HOW?

DISCUSSION INFORMATION:

The following slides will give information on HOW the teacher can support the student in each of the three roles. Move to the next slide and begin discussion.

HELP
THE STUDENT
WITH
BULLY BEHAVIOR
BY:

1. **Involve the student in a helping activity.**

2. **Offer the Behavior Change Worksheet**

3. **Give Consequences – 3 R's of Discipline***

4. **Look for positive leadership roles for the student**

5. **Refer to the class lesson summary poster, "The Roles of Bullying and What to do..."**

*adapted with permission from Barbara Colorosa (2003). The Bully, the Bullied, and the Bystander. New York, NY: HarpersCollins Publishers Inc.

DISCUSSION INFORMATION:

1. *Share the importance of strengthening empathy – caring about others – to counteract the habit or need to be mean or hurtful with the behavior. Perhaps enlist their help to work with younger students or someone with a disability. As they begin helping, make comments and compliments to strengthen a caring character. Talk about the other person's feelings and how to help.*

2. *Ask the teacher to refer to the Behavior-Change Worksheet in the folder. As you review the sheet, explain that this can be used if the student acknowledges her hurtful behavior and wants to improve. Encourage the teacher to review the steps for behavior change with the student and support them in the process.*

3. ***Share the following information with the teachers:***
   Discuss the problem with the student - do not accept excuses or blaming others- use such statements as: "We do not accept bully behavior in our class." Or when the student attempts to blame, respond, "I am talking about your behavior at this time." Impose logical consequences for the bully behavior such as remove the student from social situations (ex. lunch, recess). Utilize the 3 R's of discipline: restitution, resolution, and reconciliation which involves apologizing and fixing what he/she did, come up with a plan to keep it from happening again, and find a way to heal the hurt – perhaps inviting the other person to participate in a friend activity.

4. *Ask the teacher to consider the student's situation to see if involving the student in a healthy activity to gain appropriate attention and sense of power would be helpful.*

5. *Ask the teacher to refer to the class lesson summary poster, "The Roles of Bullying and What to do..." in the folder. Review this sheet together focusing on the Bully Behavior section. Encourage the teacher to direct the student to this poster and review the information with them. Remind the teacher that a child may be using bully behavior in one situation, but may be the victim in another.*

HELP THE TARGET SO THEY DON'T BECOME A VICTIM OF BULLYING BY:

1. **Review the difference between a conflict and bullying**

2. **Utilize the "Bully Behavior Reporting Sheet"**

3. **Clarify with the student the IN/OUT Rule***

4. **Don't rescue the target/victim; EMPOWER them. Respond by…**
   ASKING the target/victim:
   - *"Do you believe what they said?"*
   - *"What can you think or tell your self about it that would help?"*
   As the student shares a positive way to think about the situation,
   COMPLIMENT the student with a statement such as:
   - *"Sounds like a smart way to think!" or "Very mature of you!"*

   "Give a man a fish; you have fed him for today. Teach a man to fish;
   and you have fed him for a lifetime." — *source unknown*

5. **Refer to the class lesson summary poster, "The Roles of**
   Bullying and What to do…"

"Nobody can make you feel inferior without your consent." —*E. Roosevelt*

**Concept used with permission from* No Room For Bullies *(2005). Boys Town Press, Boys Town: Nebraska.*

DISCUSSION INFORMATION:

1. *Share with the teacher to clarify with the student whether the problem is a conflict (disagreement of equal power) or a bully problem (with intent to hurt and an imbalance of power). By defining the problem, it helps clarify the solution.*

2. *Ask the teacher to refer to the "Bully Behavior Reporting Sheet" in the folder. Explain that the form is provided to allow the target to think through and write down the information.*

3. *Encourage the teacher to help the student clarify if the information would be considered tattling or telling by using the guideline of the IN/OUT rule. (see previous information on page 27). Caution the teachers that when a student is telling to help someone "out" of trouble that it is important for us to take the time to deal with the problem or connect them with an adult who can.*

4. *The above information gives specifics on how to empower the target rather than to "rescue" the person. Refer to the quote.*

5. *Ask the teacher to refer students to the class lesson summary poster, "The Roles of Bullying and What to do…" to review the strategies for the target/victim.*

Read Eleanor Roosevelt's quote.

HELP THE BYSTANDER BY:

1. Clarifying with the student the **IN/OUT Rule.**[*]

2. Complimenting the student for having the courage and caring to tell.

3. Referring to the student lesson **Summary Poster, "The Roles of Bullying and What to do...".** Discuss with the bystander:
   - if and what they could say to the bully
   - what they could do to help the target
   - and how they can show the target their support

Concept used with permission from <u>No Room For Bullies</u> (2005). Boys Town Press, Boys Town: Nebraska.

DISCUSSION INFORMATION:

1. *Encourage the teachers to clarify the IN/OUT Rule (introduced previously on page 27) with the student. Ask if the student's reason for sharing is to get someone IN or OUT of trouble. If they are sharing to get someone OUT of trouble then get involved.*

2. *Encourage the teachers to compliment the student for being willing to tell. Share that it is important to compliment the student. Explain that we are assisting in the development of future citizens who care about others and are willing to help - a kind word can go a long way.*

3. *Ask the teacher to refer students to the class lesson summary poster, "The Roles of Bullying and What to do..." to review the strategies for the bystander. Encourage the teacher to help the student make a plan of ways to help in the future.*

WHAT ELSE CAN WE DO TO SUPPORT AN EFFECTIVE SCHOOLWIDE BULLYING PROGRAM?

DISCUSSION INFORMATION:

Depending on your program you tailor for your school you may include any of the following teacher-led activities to share with them:

> *Class Activity: On the Scene with Bullying*
> *Class Activity: What Would You Do If…*
> *Class Activity: What's the Meaning of This?*
> *Class Activity: Children's Literature on Bullying*
> *Class Activity: Write About It…*
> *Class Activity: Secret Pals*
> *Class Activity: Terrific Tattles/Good Gossips*

Direct the teachers to the sheets in their folders that you have included and review the activity. Explain that the activities were designed to be brief and/or to fit into the academic curriculum.

Ask for other suggestions of how to help the student

Share any upcoming school-wide plans so the teacher is aware and can support the activity. Possible school-wide plans are videos available, assembly programs, information shared on morning announcements, poster displays, etc.

> "I have come to a frightening conclusion that I am the decisive element in the classroom…As a teacher, I possess tremendous power to make a child's life miserable or joyous. I can be a tool of torture or an instrument of inspiration, can humiliate or humor, hurt or heal. In all situations, it is my response that decides whether a crisis will be escalated or de-escalated, and a child humanized or dehumanized."
>
> — Haim Ginott

TEACHERS DO MAKE A DIFFERENCE IN THE LIVES OF CHILDREN!

DISCUSSION INFORMATION:

Thank the teachers for their commitment to helping children.

HOW TEACHERS CAN HELP
IN THE THREE ROLES OF BULLYING

* ## Help the student with **BULLY BEHAVIOR** by:
- Involving the student in a helping activity to develop care and concern
- Offering the Behavior Change Worksheet for the student to complete
- Using logical consequences for the behavior such as removal from social situations (ex. lunch, recess)
- Utilizing the 3 R's of Discipline*
  <u>RESTITUTION</u> – involves apologizing and "fixing" what he/she did (if it means going to every person that you spread the rumor to and correct the information, then do so)
  <u>RESOLUTION</u> – come up with a plan to keep it from happening again
  <u>RECONCILIATION</u> – find a way to heal the hurt, perhaps inviting the other person to participate in a friend activity.
- Looking for positive leadership roles for the student to gain attention and power in appropriate ways

*Adapted with permission from Barbara Colorosa (2003). <u>The Bully, the Bullied, and the Bystander</u>. New York, NY: Harper Collins Publishers, Inc.

* ## Help the **TARGET** so they don't become a VICTIM of bullying by:
- Clarifying with the student whether the problem is a conflict (disagreement of equal power) or a bullying problem (imbalance of power with the intent to hurt). By defining the problem, it helps clarify the solution.
- Utilizing the "Bully Behavior Reporting Sheet"
- Clarifying with the student the IN/OUT Rule.* Ask if the student's reason for sharing is to get someone IN or OUT of trouble. If they are sharing to get someone OUT of trouble then get involved to help.
- Not rescuing the target/victim; EMPOWER them. Respond by…
  ASKING the target/victim:
  "Do you believe what they said?"
  "What can you think or tell yourself about it that would help?"
  As the student shares a positive way to think about the situation, COMPLIMENT the student with a statement such as:
  "Sounds like a smart way to think!" or *"Very mature of you!"*

* ## Help the **BYSTANDER** by:
- Clarifying with the student the IN/OUT Rule**
- Complimenting the student for having the courage and care to tell
- Discussing with the bystander:
  – if and what they could say to the bully
  – what they could do to help the target
  – and how they can show the target their support

Refer students to the class lesson summary poster, "The Roles of Bullying and What to do…"

*Concept used with permission from <u>No Room For Bullies</u> (2005). Boys Town Press, Boys Town: Nebraska.

BULLYING REPORT
F O R M

Date of Report: _____

If you see or experience bullying behavior including relational aggressive behavior, please complete this form and return it to your teacher.

Person making the report: _____

Homeroom Teacher: _____ Date of Incident: _____

Were you the bystander (witness) or the target/victim: _____

Is this ongoing behavior? ☐ YES or ☐ NO

Who did the bullying behavior? _____

What was the bullying behavior? _____

_____

Who was the target/victim? _____

What did the target/victim do? _____

Where did this take place? _____

Did others see this bullying behavior? If so, Who? _____

What have you tried to do to help this problem? _____

_____

Your signature: _____

SCHOOL-WIDE
APPROACH TO BULLYING

CLASS ACTIVITY:

ON THE SCENE WITH BULLYING

Purpose:
To prompt discussions on bullying

Materials Needed:
Make overhead transparencies of the following bullying scenes on pages 37-41.

Procedure:
Display each picture and discuss using such questions as:

* "What do you think is happening in this picture?"
* "Who is the Bully, the Target, the Bystander?"
* "What do you think each person is Saying? Thinking? Feeling?"
* "What could each person do to handle the situation in the best way?

Optional Activity:
Display each picture and use as a writing prompt for the student to create a story of a helpful way to deal with the situation.

In the picture _____

_____

_____

A helpful way to deal with this situation is

_____

_____

_____

ON THE SCENE
WITH BULLYING

38

ON THE SCENE
WITH BULLYING

CLASS ACTIVITY:

WHAT WOULD YOU DO IF...

Purpose:

To encourage the student to think ahead about appropriate, helpful ways to handle or deal with difficult situations.

Materials/Preparation:

Copy this sheet, cut apart the "What If" situations below, and place in a bag or box to be drawn. Add or change any of the examples depending on the needs and age of the class.

Procedures:

Ask for volunteers to select a strip of paper from the bag and read to the class. A student can lead the class in a discussion of what to THINK, SAY, or DO in the given situation.

* WHAT would you think, say, or do IF you realized you were joining in with the laughing when a friend was making fun of someone else?

* WHAT would you think, say, or do IF you were the one leading the way in encouraging your group to leave someone out?

* WHAT would you think, say, or do IF someone called you a name?

* WHAT would you think, say, or do IF someone put their hand up and rolled their eyes at you?

* WHAT would you think, say, or do IF two of your good friends were whispering and darting their eyes at you?

* WHAT would you think, say, or do IF you happened to see a note that some of the classmates wrote mean things about you?

* WHAT would you think, say, or do IF a classmate asked you to add your signature to a list that all your other classmates have already signed saying they hated a certain person?

* WHAT would you think, say, or do IF you saw a friend of yours making fun of someone else's clothes?

WHAT'S THE MEANING OF THIS?

Purpose:

To gain inspiration, support, and knowledge from famous quotes.

Materials:

Make an overhead transparency of the QUOTES page.

Procedure:

Display the overhead transparency covering up all but the particular quote to focus on. Select a student to read the quote and then encourage a class discussion on the meaning of the quote and how it can apply to our lives.

WHAT'S THE MEANING OF THIS?

QUOTES

✳ "Nobody can make you feel inferior without your consent."

—Eleanor Roosevelt

✳ "I encourage young people to refuse to let others define you."

—2003 Miss America Erika Harold

✳ "Cowardice asks the question: is it safe?
Expediency asks the question: is it politic?
Vanity asks the question: is it popular?
But conscience asks the question: is it right? And there comes a time when one must take a position that is neither safe, nor politic, nor popular – but one must take it because it's right."

—Martin Luther King Jr.

✳ "People come into our lives for a reason, a season, or a lifetime."

—source unknown

✳ "Success is to be measured not so much by the position that one has reached in life as by the obstacles one has overcome while trying to succeed."

—Booker T. Washington

✳ "The only way to have a friend is to be one."

—Ralph Waldo Emerson

✳ "America is not like a blanket… America is more like a quilt – many patches, many pieces, many colors, many sizes, all woven together and held together by a common thread."

— Jesse Jackson

✳ "We hold these truths to be self-evident: that all men are created equal."

—Thomas Jefferson

✳ "The person that has self-respect is safe from others.
That person wears a coat of armor that none can pierce."

—Henry Wadsworth Longfellow

✳ "The strong man is the man who can stand up for his rights and not hit back."

—Dr. Martin Luther King, Jr.

CHILDREN'S LITERATURE ON BULLYING

Purpose:
To use books and their stories to help children to connect to bullying situations and its roles.

Materials:
Children's Literature

The following books are examples of books that explore the topic of bullying. Always review additional books on this topic as new material continually becomes available. Boys and girls can both relate to most of the following books; however, the books listed first have a female as a main character and/or deal with typical girl bullying and the last two books listed have male main characters.

* *My Secret Bully* by T. Ludwig (Grades 3-8) Relational aggression among girls with "on again off again", friends and emotional cruelty. The victim stands up for herself assertively. Story provides opportunities for various discussions on relational aggression.

* *The English Roses* by Madonna (Grades 3-6) Portrays a girl's clique exclusion who with the help of the "fairy godmother" develop empathy and understanding of others.

* *The Recess Queen* by A. O'Neill (Grades 1-5) Fun book about the new girl, Katie Sue, that stands up to Mean Jean who is bossing and controlling. Katie Sue invites her to play – they become friends.

* *Dancing in the Wings* by K. Nelson (Grades 2-3) Story of a girl who was made fun of for being too tall with big feet. She continued her dancing and found confidence in herself and her talent.

* *Stand Tall Molly Lou Melon* by Patty Lovell (Grades 1-5) Molly is short, clumsy, and has buck teeth but she doesn't mind, her grandmother has always told her to walk proud and smile. When Molly starts a new school, a bully picks on her on the first day but Molly knows just what to do – walk proud and smile.

* *Say Something* by Peggy Moss (Grades 2-6) Story of a girl who watches other people get teased/bullied and she feels sorry for them. When she gets teased herself she realizes that the bystander needs to DO something to help.

* *Mr. Peabodies Apples* by Madonna (Grades 3-8) A story of how rumors can cause damage. Baseball player started a rumor about a teacher and the bystanders became participants by passing the rumor.

* *Alley Oops* by Janice Levy (Grades 3-6) The story focuses on the bully, JJ Fox, who is being corrected by his father for his bullying behavior. His father speaks of himself as being a bully when he was young and that the boy he picked on is now grown and powerful. He regrets his earlier behavior. The story continues with JJ changing his bullying behavior and becoming friends.

Procedure:
Enjoy reading the book to the class and discuss the story. The following questions may help guide the discussion. You may also add the perspective footprints on p. 48, Encourage students to take turns standing on the different footprints – bully, target, bystander – as they discuss the different perspectives of the story.

CHILDREN'S LITERATURE ON BULLYING BEHAVIOR QUESTIONS FOR REVIEWING

1. Book Title: _____

2. Who were the main characters in the story? _____
_____

3. What type of **bullying behavior** happened in the story? _____
_____

4. How did the **target/victim** of bullying feel about the bullying? _____
_____

5. Were there **bystanders** in the story and if so what did they do? _____
_____

6. Did the characters handle the bullying well? Explain. _____
_____

7. Would you have handled the bullying differently? If so, what would you

have done? _____

_____

8. What did you learn from the story? _____

CLASS ACTIVITY: FOOTPRINT PERSPECTIVE

Purpose:
To provide a structured activity to review the different perspectives in a bully situation.

Materials:
Make three copies of the set of footprints on page 48.
    (May choose to copy on different color cardstock)
Add one of the following labels to each set of footprints:
    Bully Behavior (Aggressor), Target/Victim, Bystander

Procedure:
Present a bullying situation through story telling, reading a book, looking at a picture, or reading a story written by students. Place the three sets of footprints on the floor and allow students to stand in the footprint and retell the story from the perspective of the person listed on the footprints. Explore the thoughts and feelings of that person's perspective. Have the student change footprints for different perspectives. After having discussed all perspectives with the different thoughts and feelings, encourage the students to retell the story differently taking into consideration everyone's feelings.

Allow the footprints to remain in the classroom. This activity can be used for the class to process together a bully situation shared from students or can be used with individuals who are experiencing a bully situation.

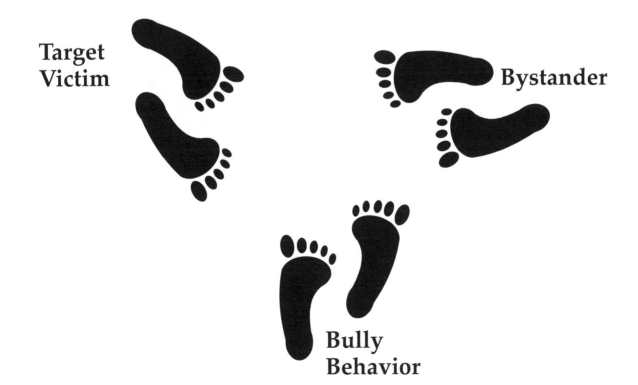

SCHOOL-WIDE APPROACH TO BULLYING

FOOTPRINT PERSPECTIVE

Directions:

Make three copies of the set of footprints below and add one of the following labels to each set of footprints: Bully Behavior (Aggressor), Target/Victim, Bystander. Encourage students to take turns standing on the different footprints as they discuss the different perspectives of a situation or story.

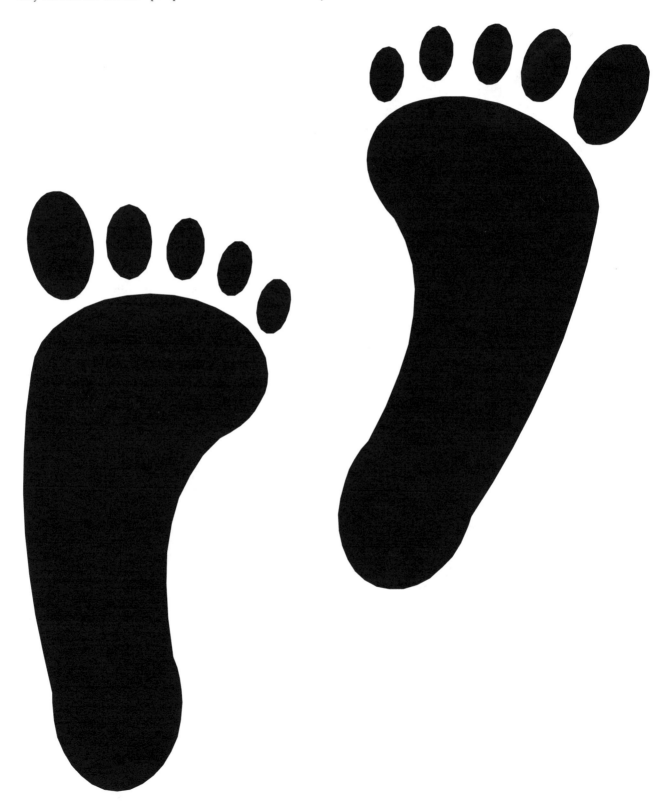

WRITE ABOUT IT...

To allow the individual student to focus on a situation of bullying allowing the student to re-write life with a better ending on paper in hopes that the process will encourage our re-writing our life for the better for real.

Procedure:

Assign to the students to create a story in writing using the topic or story starter selected. Suggestions are given below:

TOPICS

* Create a story of bullying from the point of view of the target/victim or the bystander.

* First create a story of bullying from the point of view of the bully and then add an ending in which the bully chooses better behavior.

* Ask the students to write a story about bullying in which the victim and/or the bystanders do not make good choices in handling. (May want to add some parameters). Review these papers for appropriateness to share with the class. Next distribute the selected papers to a pair of students different from the original authors, asking them to discuss appropriate, helpful ways the victim and/or bystanders could handle the problem and then to re-write the ending.

STORY STARTERS

* It happened one day. I was standing at my locker with my friend who unexpectedly turned and said to the new girl walking down the hall, "You don't belong in this school. Go back where you came from."

* The cheerleading team at our school knew that I was the best at cheering and that I have great gymnastic skills – that's why they choose me as the head cheerleader. I knew what was best for the squad, so I chose all the routines, told the other girls what they could and could not do, and was on their case all of the time about how they could do better. Over the summer I attended the national cheerleading camp. Others didn't think I was that great of a cheerleader, in fact they were bossing me around telling me that what I was doing was wrong and how I need to do better. Some of the girls at camp wouldn't let me sit with them and hang out with them during our free time. It didn't feel good. It was at that moment that I realized how I had treated and used bully behavior with my own squad back at school, I felt even worse. I decided to...

* Use the bullying situations in the class lesson chapter of this book for writing prompts.

SCHOOL-WIDE
APPROACH TO BULLYING

CLASS ACTIVITY:

SECRET PALS

Purpose:

To encourage students to show care and concern for others in doing kind deeds.

Materials:

List of student's names folded on pieces of paper and placed in a bag. Chart paper/marker for a brainstorming list.

Procedure:

Ask the students to share ways that they as students can show care and concern for each other – what would be some kind deeds that they could do?

Write their examples on chart paper or the board. Examples may include such ideas as:

* Write a friendly note to the person.
* Sit with the person at lunch, talking to get to know each other.
* Smile and be friendly.
* Ask them about their day and be a good listener.
* Look for and compliment the person on things they do well.
* Include the person in activities.

Assign each student to a "secret pal" by having them draw a classmates name from the bag. Explain that they are not to tell the person or anyone else whose name they have drawn, but are to do acts of kindness for that person during the week. Display the chart paper of kind deeds for a reference.

At the end of the week *allow* students to take turns guessing **who** their secret pal may be and **why**. Ask that the "real secret pal of ____ please stand up."

Kind Deeds
1. Share a smile.
2. Be a good listener.
3. Write a kind note.

Purpose:

To encourage students to look for the good in others and to talk and share about people's successes and positive things rather than their defeats.

Materials:

A small soft ball for tossing in the classroom

Procedure:

Set aside time each day for students to tell good things about other classmates.

Use the ball to structure this sharing time. Begin by tossing the ball to one student. The student who the ball was tossed to must tell something good about someone else in the class – perhaps something they saw that the person do or something they are good at.

Next they are to toss the ball to another classmate who is to share a "terrific tattle" about someone.

To encourage classmates to be tuned in and listening, when a ball is tossed to someone you may change the instruction and ask them to do a "good gossip" and repeat the nice thing that the previous student just said about someone. Point out that it's okay to pass on good information about people.

As the teacher, please include yourself in the "terrific tattles". Your sincere, good statements about others may set a more positive, serious tone for the activity. If you suspect a classmate as being one who may start or spread inappropriate rumors, you may select that person for you to give a positive, sincere compliment to as you hold the ball before you toss it to the first student.

SCHOOL-WIDE ACTIVITIES
To Promote Anti-Bullying/Anti-Relational Aggression

Purpose:

To continually provide reminders of the anti-bullying/ anti-relational aggression promotion.

Suggestions:

* Assembly Programs inviting speakers from the area

* Videos on bullying shown school-wide or for individual check-out

* Anti-Bullying or Anti-RA poster contest

* Mix it up lunch day where students are encouraged to sit and eat lunch with someone different. Check the website: www.mixitup.org for more information.

SCHOOL-WIDE ACTIVITY

COMMERCIALS
for a BULLY-FREE SCHOOL

Purpose:

To provide a creative way to "catch" the students' attention to focus on the topic of bullying.

Procedure:

Commercials can be used during televised morning announcements or individually in classrooms or school-wide assembly programs.

You may choose to first use the commercials given and then encourage classes/students to write their own commercials on the topic of a bully-free school.

SCHOOL-WIDE
APPROACH TO BULLYING

COMMERCIAL: BULLY-FREE SCENES

Props Needed:

Posterboard or box outline of a school with the words boldly written on the front "BULLY-FREE SCHOOL", and several school books. Need four actors.

Announcer:

Get it here, your BULLY-FREE SCHOOL *(hold up the outline of the school)*. It makes you feel safe, good, and proud of yourself and others. *(pause)* Tired of those unsightly scenes of... *(camera goes to three students briefly acting out the following scenes:)*

Scene 1: *Bully calling someone a name, Bystander laughing, Victim has their eyes down and appears with hurt feelings*

Scene 2: *Bully rolling their eyes with their hand up in a mean way toward the victim. Victim has their eyes down and appears to be hurt.*

While the scenes are being acted out the announcer needs to label the scenes with the following words) Name-calling, laughing, and eye rolling!

Announcer continues:

Instead it's time to show our CARE and CONCERN for others by... *(camera goes to three students briefly acting out the following scenes:)*

Scene 1: *2 people encouraging the third person to join their group – all are happy and smiling.*

Scene 2: *1 person is helping another person pick up dropped books.
While the scenes are being acted out the announcer needs to label the scenes with the following words) Including a friend in an activity and helping someone out.*

Announcer concludes:

Our choice is a Bully-Free school **(hold up/point to the outline of the school).**

COMMERCIAL: BULLY-FREE SCHOOL

Props Needed:

Box in the shape of a school with Bully Free School written on the outside.

Three strips of poster board with the following information written that can be pulled from the school box and shared:

If you have **BULLY BEHAVIOR**– admit it and change.

If you are a **TARGET** – be assertive, say STOP! and be proud of who you are.

If you are a **BYSTANDER** – be a friend to help or tell.

Need one actor

Announcer:

(hold up the school box)

Get it here your Bully-Free School. Let's look inside to see the skills needed.

(open the doors of the school house and pull out the 'bully' strip first, show, and read)

If you have BULLY BEHAVIOR – admit it and change.

(Next pull out the second strip about the 'target' – show and read)

If you are a TARGET – be assertive, say STOP! and be proud of who you are.

(Then pull out the third strip about the 'bystander' – show and read)

If you are a BYSTANDER – be a friend to help or tell. Well, you heard it here first!

COMMERCIAL: REAL LIFE

Props Needed:

Two actors (one actor, playing the role of the target, needs to be unemotional, speaking in monotone and the other person needs to pretend to be the professional actor speaking with excitement and intrigue)

Voice Over:

(Camera can focus on the two actors who remain motionless as the voice over talks)
We are enacting a real life situation of bullying in which a good way to handle was chosen. Since the person telling the story is a 'regular person' we have asked a professional actor to help Mary tell her story. Camera's ready? Action!

Mary:

(Speaking with no emotions with a 'flat' voice) One day I was walking down the hall at school when

Professional actor:

Mary was dodging students down the hall, rushing to her next class, stressing about her Math assignment when

Mary:

My best friend from last year called from across the hall and yelled: "Mary is such a jerk" the people with her laughed. I thought oh, well and kept walking.

Professional actor:

When I heard those cutting words I felt crushed and hurt. I wanted to crawl in a hole and hide. But then I remembered the importance of not letting the bullying words bother us so I stopped to appreciate my good qualities, pulled my courage together, held my head high with a smile, and pledged to have a good day.

Voice Over:

(Mary and the professional actor freeze – are motionless as the voice over speaks) So that's Mary's story – what about your story? Do you have the confidence to value yourself when others are mean to you?

GIVE A HAND FOR GOOD DEEDS

Smile and be friendly

Help someone

Make a point to include others

Show respect

Say nice things about and to others

Encourage another person

SCHOOL-WIDE ACTIVITY

WALL DISPLAYS TO PROMOTE A BULLY-FREE SCHOOL

PUT A STOP TO BULLYING

STOP rumors

STOP eye rolling

STOP excluding

STOP name-calling

STOP threatening

STOP teasing

STOP hitting, pushing, kicking, tripping

STOP hurtful messages by text or computer

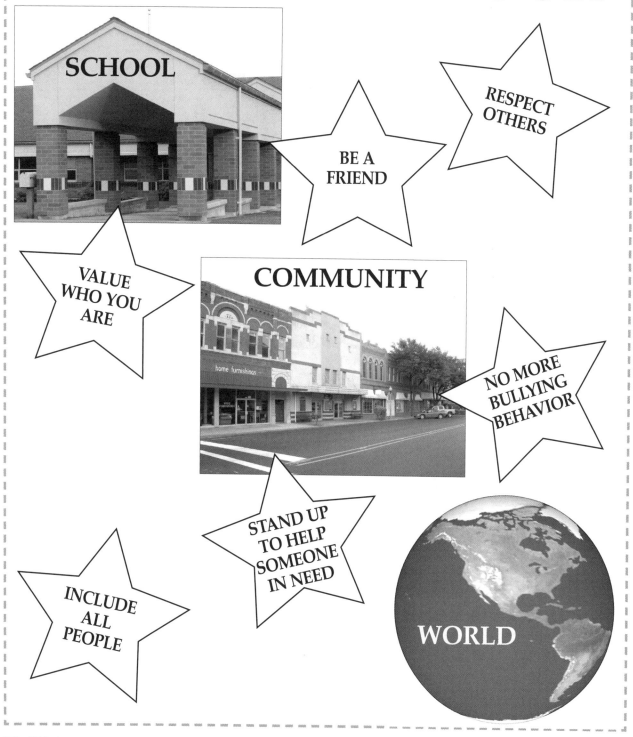

YOU CAN MAKE A DIFFERENCE IN OUR

SCHOOL

BE A FRIEND

RESPECT OTHERS

VALUE WHO YOU ARE

COMMUNITY

NO MORE BULLYING BEHAVIOR

STAND UP TO HELP SOMEONE IN NEED

INCLUDE ALL PEOPLE

WORLD

SCHOOL-WIDE APPROACH TO BULLYING

SCHOOL-WIDE APPROACH TO BULLYING

STEPS FOR A BULLY-FREE SCHOOL

If you have
BULLY BEHAVIOR
– admit it and
change.

If you are a **BYSTANDER** –
be a friend to help or tell.

If you are a **TARGET** –
be assertive, say **STOP!**
and be proud of who you are.

CHAPTER 2

Class Lessons on Bullying

CLASS LESSONS

Classroom guidance provides a unique opportunity to share information with all students. The four lessons in this chapter deal with all types of bullying - both direct and indirect. The examples given in the lessons include bullying through the more physical aggressive type of hitting, pushing, shoving to the emotional bullying of threatening, name-calling, and hurtful teasing, to the social bullying (relational aggression) of exclusions, eye-rolling, bossing, controlling, manipulation, and spreading rumors. Acknowledging that classrooms are typically composed of both girls and boys, the lessons on bullying will include examples of both boys and girls involved with the direct and indirect bullying.

Four class lessons on bullying are included in this chapter. Please feel free to change or vary the lesson to meet your style and the needs of your students. Each lesson also includes a summary poster and parent letter. It is the belief that teaching typically takes more than just a 30-minute one time lesson on the topic, therefore the teaching is extended through a visual reminder of a summary poster of the lesson as well as a follow-up parent letter for home reinforcement. The **summary poster**/visual reminder provides a tool for teachers to direct students' attention to the poster when situations arise that are pertinent. Learning is achieved when the student can connect information presented to real life situations. An additional reinforcement for learning is the **parent letter**. The purpose of the parent letter is to update the home on information shared so that both home and school can be talking the same language and reinforcing the skills introduced. Suggestions and activities for home reinforcement are included in each letter. When different aspects of the student's life are working together – school and home – success for learning is increased.

The class lessons on bullying are:

CLASS LESSONS

BULLYING –
WHAT'S IT ALL ABOUT?

Purpose:
To understand that bullying includes both direct and indirect methods, includes three roles (bully behavior, target/victim, and bystanders), and the lesson provides suggestions on what to do for each of the three roles.

Estimated Time:
30-45 minutes

Materials Needed:
Create overhead transparencies or scan/type the information in the boxes on pages 64-86. for a power point presentation.

Copy of the Summary Poster for each class

Copy of the Parent Letter and the "Roles of Bullying and What to Do..." Sheet for each student

Procedure:
Display the overhead or power point presentation created from pages 64-86. Use the Discussion Information located at the bottom of each page as a discussion guideline, asking questions and adding additional information.

Summary Poster:
Copy and display in the classroom the summary poster on page 87. The poster is intended to be a visual reminder for the students and a tool for the teacher in reinforcing the lesson and for connecting the learning to real life situations.

Parent Letter:
Copy the parent letter along with the "Roles of Bullying and What to Do..." sheet for each student to take home. The parent letter is intended to update the home on information shared so the school and home can work together to reinforce the information/skills presented.

CLASS LESSONS

BULLYING

WHAT'S IT ALL ABOUT?

DISCUSSION INFORMATION:

Read the topic and move to the next slide

RAISE YOUR HAND IF YOU HAVE EVER BULLIED SOMEONE.

DISCUSSION INFORMATION:

Typically no one or only one or two students will raise their hand.
Simply nod your head and move to the next slide.

WHAT IS A BULLY?

NAME SOME BULLYING BEHAVIORS.

DISCUSSION INFORMATION:

Call on raised hands as students share their thoughts. Repeat or reframe their answers as necessary to summarize.

A PERSON USING BULLY BEHAVIOR IS SOMEONE WHO HURTS SOMEONE ELSE BY INTENTIONALLY PUSHING OR HITTING.

DISCUSSION INFORMATION:

Ask the students to share what they think is happening in the picture. Discuss how the person getting pushed or hit may feel.

A PERSON USING BULLY BEHAVIOR IS SOMEONE WHO THREATENS YOU WITH A FIST IN YOUR FACE.

DISCUSSION INFORMATION:

Allow time to read and view the picture and then move to the next slide.

A PERSON USING BULLY BEHAVIOR IS SOMEONE WHO TEASES WITH MEAN WORDS.

DISCUSSION INFORMATION:

Ask the students to explain what is happening in the picture.
Ask them to share how the student may feel about the teasing.

A PERSON USING BULLY BEHAVIOR IS ALSO SOMEONE WHO JOINS IN THE LAUGHING WHEN SOMEONE ELSE TEASES.

DISCUSSION INFORMATION:

Ask the students to share what they see happening in this picture. Point out the joining in with laughing at what someone said in making fun of someone is hurtful and also becomes a bullying behavior.

Ask where the teacher is. (Point out that the teacher on recess duty has her back to the girls and doesn't hear the situation. Explain that most bullying will happen when an adult is not in "earshot".

A PERSON USING BULLY BEHAVIOR IS ALSO SOMEONE WHO MAKES A POINT NOT TO LET YOU SIT WITH THEM AT LUNCH.

DISCUSSION INFORMATION:

Discuss the picture pointing out that if a person is left out on purpose then it is hurtful behavior and is considered bullying behavior.

A PERSON USING BULLY BEHAVIOR IS ALSO SOMEONE WHO EXCLUDES OTHERS FROM THEIR GROUP OR ACTIVITY.

DISCUSSION INFORMATION:

Ask the students to share what is happening in the picture. Discuss the feelings involved.

A PERSON USING BULLY BEHAVIOR IS ALSO SOMEONE WHO HURTS YOUR FEELINGS ON PURPOSE BY ROLLING THEIR EYES AT YOU.

DISCUSSION INFORMATION:

Ask the students if they have ever rolled their eyes at someone. Explain that if it is done in a hurtful way then it is also bullying behavior.

A PERSON USING BULLY BEHAVIOR IS SOMEONE WHO USES THEIR POPULARITY TO BOSS OTHERS AROUND, TELLING OTHERS WHAT THEY SHOULD OR SHOULDN'T DO.

DISCUSSION INFORMATION:

Ask: What do you think is happening in the picture?

How would you handle the situation if it happened to you?

Why do you think the person is using the bossing/controlling behavior?

A PERSON USING BULLY BEHAVIOR IS SOMEONE WHO TRIES TO CONTROL THEIR FRIEND AND NOT LET THEM SPEND TIME WITH OTHERS.

DISCUSSION INFORMATION:

Ask: What do you think is happening in this picture?

A PERSON USING BULLY BEHAVIOR IS SOMEONE WHO SPREADS BAD RUMORS ABOUT OTHERS.

DISCUSSION INFORMATION:

Explain that the comment about her friend liking Bert is not a true statement.

Ask: Why do you think she said it if it wasn't true? (Point out that her first statement indicates that she is mad at her friend – is there a chance she made up something untrue just to get back at her for something?

Ask: Is it a right thing to do? Emphasize that spreading rumors is a bullying behavior.

A PERSON USING BULLY BEHAVIOR IS SOMEONE WHO GOSSIPS OR REPEATS BAD RUMORS ABOUT OTHERS.

DISCUSSION INFORMATION:

Ask the students why they think we gossip and are tempted to repeat rumors. (Answers may include: to get attention, to have something to talk about, to gain power and popularity with others for the juicy gossip we bring to the group.)

RAISE YOUR HAND NOW IF YOU THINK YOU HAVE USED BULLY BEHAVIOR.

Let's look at the behaviors we need to add to our bully behaviors list.

IT'S NOT OKAY TO:

Push, hit, hurt others physically, threaten, intimidate

AND IT'S ALSO NOT OKAY TO:

- Tease in a hurtful way
- Join in laughing when someone else is making fun of someone
- Exclude others from the group or activities
- Roll our eyes intending to hurt
- Boss our friends, telling them what they can or can't do
- Control and manipulate others
- Spread rumors about others

DISCUSSION INFORMATION:

Typically more if not all students raise their hand now.

Share the following: A bully is not just that person out there that threatens, intimidates and hits people. We can be the bully when we exclude people, spread rumors, gossip, or join in and laugh at someone who is being teased. When we make this poor choice to hurt others we are using bullying behavior. I am proud of you for having the courage to admit that you have had that bullying behavior. We can only work to change something after we recognize it as a problem and admit that we are doing it. So let's look at the definition of Bullying.

DEFINITION:

BULLYING
is a pattern of repeated behavior that is meant to hurt someone (physically, emotionally, or socially) and usually has an imbalance of power (physical or social).

DISCUSSION INFORMATION:

Emphasize the repeated behavior that is meant to be hurtful. Point out that if someone truly accidentally trips and bumps into you then that is not bullying because there was no intent to harm. Or if two people are equally fussing over whose turn it is – that is a conflict not bullying and conflict management skills need to be used.

Explain the different types of the imbalance of power as:
> ***Physically*** *– one person bigger or stronger than the other*

> ***Socially*** *– one person is perceived to have more social power than the other or perhaps skilled more verbally to out talk the person.*

DID THE PICTURES WE LOOKED AT A MOMENT AGO STIR UP ANY THOUGHTS OF?

Oh... I've acted like that before...

Yeah...that's happened to me before.

I saw that happening to someone else.

DISCUSSION INFORMATION:

Typically students will nod their heads and agree that they have experienced each of the three listed.

Move to the next slide as you say that there are three roles in the bullying situation.

CLASS LESSONS

80

© YouthLight, Inc.

3 ROLES IN A BULLYING SITUATION

The **Aggressor** is the one doing the Bullying Behavior

The **Target or Victim** is the person being bullied

The **Bystander** is the person watching/seeing the bullying happen

DISCUSSION INFORMATION:

If time allows, have students share personal stories without indicating specific names.

DO YOU THINK GIRLS TYPICALLY BULLY DIFFERENTLY THAN BOYS?

HOW?

DISCUSSION INFORMATION:

Summarize the students' answers. If the following did not come out in the discussion, add:

Both boys and girls can exhibit direct and indirect bullying behavior. However, boys typically are more direct about their bullying, gaining their power with pushing, shoving, and threatening. On the other hand, since girls typically gain their identities through friendships and social relationships, they are more likely to engage in indirect forms of bullying such as spreading rumors, controlling, manipulating, and exclusion. Their bullying is motivated by either fear of not being a part of a group or to gain power and prestige in a desired group. The above reasons are not acceptable. Bullying is not okay. It is never okay to intentionally and repeatedly hurt another person.

Introduce the next slide by saying: "Now we know what bullying behavior looks like and we have talked about the three roles of bullying and how we have been in all three of those roles at one time or other, the next step is to talk about what to do when we are in each of those roles." Let the student know that they will be receiving a summary sheet of the information shared in the next three slides of the "What to do…".

WHAT TO DO WHEN YOU ARE THE BYSTANDER:

(Choosing to ignore the bullying is the same as supporting the behavior)

1. **Refuse to be an audience for the bullying incident**
2. **If appropriate and safe, ask the bully to stop (Use words like, "Knock it off!" or "Cut it out!")**
3. **Be a friend to the victim, invite them to talk with you (Say, "Come play on our team." or "Can I sit with you at lunch?")**
4. **Support the victim – write the victim a note or tell him/her that you don't agree with the bully**
5. **Tell an adult (There is a difference between TATTLING and TELLING: The IN/OUT Rule*)**

*Concept used with permission from <u>No Room For Bullies</u> (2005). Boys Town Press, Boys Town: Nebraska.

DISCUSSION INFORMATION:

Remind the student that the bystander is the person standing by that witnesses or sees the bullying happening. Explain that bystanders have a great deal of power in the bullying situations – power to make a difference.

Ask the students if any of the following responses by the bystander will help the bullying and make a difference:
- *You see someone being bullied and you become afraid yourself that you might be the next victim so you stay quiet and hope it doesn't happen to you. Will it help?*
- *You choose to ignore it because you see it happen all of the time so you think it's a normal part of life. Will that help?*
- *You stand and watch or join in and laugh about the bullying? Will that help?*

Let the student know that they need to find their courage to do something and make a difference. Review and discuss each strategy in the slide.
Add for the following strategies:
   #2 – Explain that if the bully is older and much bigger, you may choose not to talk to the bully – move on to another strategy. However, if the bully is a friend that you have power with and the person may listen to you, then ask the bully to stop.
   *#5 – Explain the IN and OUT rule as: If something is wrong and you are trying to get someone **OUT** of trouble then you need to tell, but if you are trying to get someone **IN** trouble then don't tell – that's tattling.*

WHAT TO DO WHEN YOU HAVE BULLY BEHAVIOR:

1. **Realize and identify the problem behavior.**

2. **Acknowledge that you need to change the behavior.**

3. **Apologize for the negative behavior.**

4. **Use the Bully Behavior Change Worksheet.**

5. **Use your conflict management skills to handle the problem.**

6. **Increase your empathy and concern for others.**

7. **Use your leadership skills to help rather than hurt.**

DISCUSSION INFORMATION:

Compliment the student on their willingness to recognize that they have some bullying behaviors that need changing. Explain that we are human and make mistakes but it is the willingness to change that makes us a better person.

Review the 7 strategies to help. Add additional information for the following:
 #4 Refer to the Bully Behavior Change Worksheet on page 93.
   You may choose to show and review the sheet if time allows.
 #5 Summarize the conflict management skills of: "I" messages, take turns, compromise, ignore, get the facts, apologize, humor, share, or get help.

WHAT TO DO WHEN YOU ARE THE TARGET...
SO YOU DON'T BECOME THE VICTIM

1. Use your assertive skills to tell the person to stop.

2. Don't believe the bully – the bully only has the power if you give it.

3. Value yourself.

4. Report bullying incidents that are harmful, dangerous, or destructive.

5. Find safe places and people.

6. Make new friends and try new activities.

DISCUSSION INFORMATION:

Impress that we can all be a "target" of bullying at times but that if we choose not to let the bullying hurt us, then we do not become a "victim".

Review all strategies.

YOU CAN MAKE A DIFFERENCE IN OUR SCHOOL, OUR COMMUNITY, OUR WORLD.

YOU CAN HELP BY:

- Reviewing your own behavior (if there is bullying behavior then change).

- Not allowing yourself to be a victim of bullying behavior.

- Helping when you see a bullying problem.

DISCUSSION INFORMATION:

Hand out to each student the lesson follow-up parent letter and "The Roles of Bullying and What to Do..." sheet. Encourage them to post this sheet in their room, their notebook – somewhere they can keep it and refer to it.

The Roles of Bullying and What To Do...

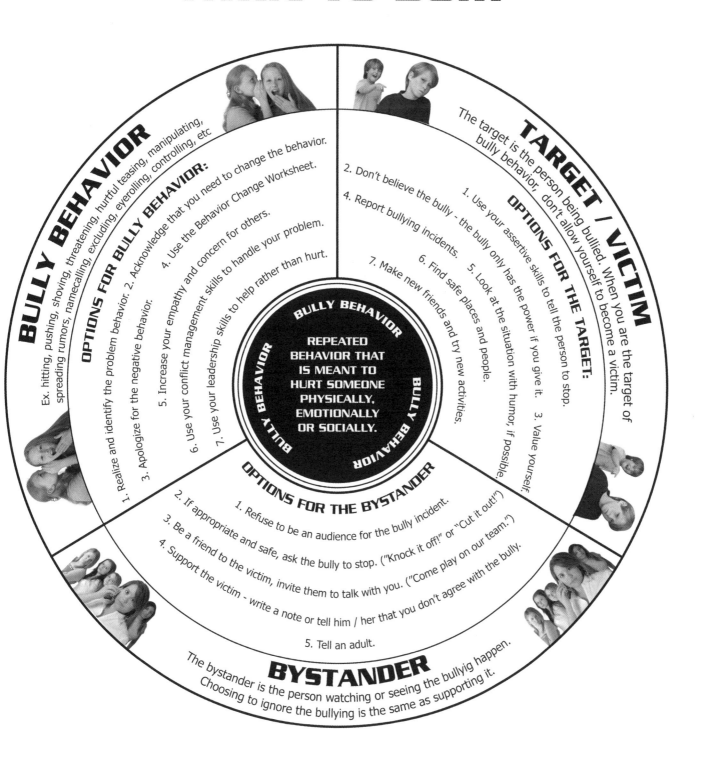

BULLY BEHAVIOR

Ex. hitting, pushing, shoving, threatening, hurtful teasing, manipulating, spreading rumors, namecalling, excluding, eyerolling, controlling, etc

OPTIONS FOR BULLY BEHAVIOR:

1. Realize and identify the problem behavior.
2. Acknowledge that you need to change the behavior.
3. Apologize for the negative behavior.
4. Use the Behavior Change Worksheet.
5. Increase your empathy and concern for others.
6. Use your conflict management skills to handle your problem.
7. Use your leadership skills to help rather than hurt.

TARGET / VICTIM

The target is the person being bullied. When you are the target of bully behavior, don't allow yourself to become a victim.

OPTIONS FOR THE TARGET:

1. Use your assertive skills to tell the person to stop.
2. Don't believe the bully - the bully only has the power if you give it.
3. Value yourself.
4. Report bullying incidents.
5. Look at the situation with humor, if possible.
6. Find safe places and people.
7. Make new friends and try new activities.

BULLY BEHAVIOR

REPEATED BEHAVIOR THAT IS MEANT TO HURT SOMEONE PHYSICALLY, EMOTIONALLY OR SOCIALLY.

OPTIONS FOR THE BYSTANDER

1. Refuse to be an audience for the bully incident.
2. If appropriate and safe, ask the bully to stop. ("Knock it off!" or "Cut it out!")
3. Be a friend to the victim, invite them to talk with you. ("Come play on our team.")
4. Support the victim - write a note or tell him / her that you don't agree with the bully.
5. Tell an adult.

BYSTANDER

The bystander is the person watching or seeing the bullyig happen. Choosing to ignore the bullying is the same as supporting it.

CLASS LESSONS

Dear Parent,

This past week our class lesson focused on Bullying. We came to the understanding that bullying behavior can be physical – hitting, pushing, shoving, threatening but it can also be the social/emotional hurt of name-calling, eye-rolling, excluding, hurtful teasing, bossing, manipulation, control, spreading rumors, etc. We discussed how girls can bully differently than boys. The reality we concluded is that we have been guilty of some type of bullying behavior and it is not an okay behavior. We defined Bullying as a pattern of repeated mean behavior that is intended to hurt someone else (physically, emotionally, or socially) and usually involves an imbalance of power – physical or social. We explored that there are 3 roles to bullying – the bully behavior, the target/victim, and the bystander. At different times in our lives we have played and will play all three of these roles; therefore, it's important to learn what to do and how to help.

When we find ourselves exhibiting **bully behavior**, the first step is to identify the problem and acknowledge that we need to work on the problem. We referenced a Behavior Change Worksheet that involves identifying the behavior to change, finding the courage to apologize, making a plan for change that includes picturing yourself with the improved behavior, writing yourself reminder notes/pictures, recording progress on a calendar or in a journal, asking for support from a friend or adult you trust, and celebrating your successes.

As we talked about the role of the **target/victim**, we pointed out that even though we may be a "target of bullying" at times, if we choose to handle it in a positive way and not allow it to bother us we can choose not to become a "victim of bullying". As adults, we can help our children by assisting in building their confidence and value in who they are and in helping our children engage in activities in which they find success.

Bystanders have a great deal of power in this situation and are encouraged to make a difference. No longer is it okay to stand by saying nothing and watch someone else get hurt, no longer is it okay not to care, no longer is it okay to join in and laugh with the bully. Each child has the power to make a difference in our school and in our world by being there and caring about other people.

Strategies of "What to do if you are the bystander….the target/victim…. and when you have bully behavior" is included on the attached summary sheet.

I appreciate your support as we work to help our children grow up to be safe, confident adults. We will continue with a school-wide emphasis of information and activities throughout the year on being a "Bully Free" School. Please call if you would like further information on the topic of bullying or have suggestions that would be helpful for our school.

Sincerely,

School Counselor

WHAT'S IN YOUR HEART?

Purpose:

To encourage the student to review their behavior and make changes working toward being kind and caring to others

Estimated Time:

30-45 minutes

Materials Needed:

Large plastic heart container that can be opened (if unable to locate use a shoe box and place a red construction paper heart on the top)

Copy "Does it Belong in Your Heart?" p. 91-92. Cut apart the strips and place in the heart container

Paper hearts for each student

Procedure:

1. Display the heart container and ask, "What comes to mind when you think of a heart?" Acknowledge and summarize the answers. Focus on the heart being the symbol of care and love. Further point out the heart is the essence of who we are – it stands for life – without the heart beating we are not living.

2. Point out that life is precious and valuable, not something to take for granted. Share that we want to make sure we live our life being the best that we can. Ask the students how they would like someone to describe their life. As students share, you may want to use the example of the story/movie Scrooge by Dickens where he had a chance, after the visits from the three spirits, to change his life to be a better person. We could say he had a change of heart!

3. Open the heart. Tell the students that we are going to see what's in this heart. Pair the students and allow each pair to blindly select a strip of paper from the heart. Explain to the students that they are to read the situation on their paper and discuss, they are to decide if it is something that we would be proud to have in our heart or not and explain why or why not.

4. Allow the students to share their situation and conclusions. If the situation is something proud to have in our heart, place the slip back inside. If it is not, add it to the trash can to get rid of it.

CLASS LESSONS

5. Ask each student to take a quiet moment to review their own lives and their behavior choices. Add the following questions to the board or read out loud to help them review.

* Have I done something this past week, above and beyond, to help someone else?
* Have I said something nice to someone this week?
* Have I said or done something that was intended to hurt another person?
* Are there some behaviors that I want to work on to have a 'change of heart' for the better?

6. Hand each student a paper heart. Ask the students to share examples of things people say or do that are intended to hurt others. Ask the students to fold their heart once for each example shared. Next, ask the student to unfold their paper heart and straighten it out – removing the folds or wrinkles. Point out the impossible task of removing all wrinkles from the heart. Relate how it is impossible to remove or "take back" hurtful words or deeds once said or done.*

7. Make the statement, "Don't be someone's wrinkle in the heart." Discuss behaviors we may want to change. Applaud their courage to admit and to work on improving. Show the Behavior Change Worksheet on page 93 and talk through the steps necessary. Make the sheet available.

Summary Poster:
Copy and display in the classroom the summary poster on p. 94. The poster is intended to be a visual reminder for the students and a tool for the teacher in reinforcing the lesson and for connecting the learning to real life situations.

Parent Letter:
Copy the parent letter on page 95 for each student to take home. The parent letter is intended to update the home on information shared so the school and home can work together to reinforce the information/skills presented.

* Wrinkled/folded Heart Analogy - source unknown

CLASS LESSONS

90

© YouthLight, Inc.

DOES IT BELONG IN YOUR HEART?

Directions:

Copy and cut apart each strip, then add them to the heart container. Next ask each pair of students to draw a slip from the heart container, to read and discuss between themselves if the situation on their paper is something they would be proud to have in their heart or not, and then take turns sharing their thoughts with the class. Either throw away the slip of paper or add back to the heart depending on if it is a behavior we would want to keep or not.

I was really mad that Jillian didn't invite me to her party so I made up an untrue rumor about her liking this really weird guy and then I told Cindy because I was sure she would pass it on.

I had to keep up my reputation as being a tough guy so when Frank walked by I laughed and said, "There goes super geek with your nerdy glasses and shirt that looks like you slept in it." My other friends joined in laughing with me and I maintained my reputation.

Michael was threatening to hurt George. I walk over and encourage Michael to leave George alone and go to class.

The teacher was at the door of the classroom busy talking with someone, Caroline was at the board working on a math problem but kept making mistakes and couldn't get it. Jackson whispered loudly, "Caroline is so dumb, she can't even count the toes on her own feet." I joined in and laughed with half of the class. Caroline's face turned red.

I walked away when my friends started gossiping about Heather.

I saw the new student trying to find a table of students to eat lunch with but only found eye-rolls and attitude. When the new student walked past our table I invited her to join our friends at the table.

The most popular girl in Science class got paired with me to do the assigned project. I was looking forward to getting to know her better and being able to hangout some. We scheduled times to get together to work on the project but she never showed and always seemed to have an excuse. Two days before the project she called me and said a lot of nice things about me and how smart I was and that if I didn't mind doing the project I could just sign her name to it and it would be okay with her. She also said that maybe we could hang out sometime together. I liked the positive attention from her and all the nice things she said so I said, "Sure, I'll do the project and just put your name on it."

I didn't like my friend Angie spending so much time with Sara - I was getting left out. So, on the computer when we were emailing back and forth, I tricked Sara into saying something not so nice about Angie and then I forwarded it on to Angie.

In our group the girls started talking bad about Jana's volleyball playing and how she was missing all the blocks. I joined in and said, "I got to go to the away game last week and Jana actually did a good job with her blocks and it looked like she added some power to her serves. I guess we all have on and off games. Hey, did you get that math assignment last night?"

The teacher embarrassed me in class about not knowing the math. Out of the corner of my eye, I thought that brainy-act Henry smiled making fun of me in class, so out in the hall at the change of classes I pushed Henry against the locker and said, "I'll get you for that!"

Melanie was sad sitting by herself about to cry so I went over to her to help. As I sat and listened, it turned out that Lauren had been mean to her. I reassured Melanie that she was a good person who many people liked.

Elizabeth, who had a lot of power in our group, was bossy about telling me where to sit. I said, "No, thank you." I turned and sat with a group of friends I hadn't seen in awhile. I enjoyed talking with them.

A classmate passes me a petition that says, "I agree to hate Danielle and exclude her from all activities." I looked at it and thought, "These are my good friends asking me to sign this, but even though I don't know Danielle that well, I don't have a problem with her. It wouldn't be right to sign it – I wouldn't want someone to do this to me." So, I said to my friend with the petition, "No way, I'd have to be crazy to sign something that mean!"

I try to get to know people who look, dress, or speak differently from me. I want to get to know who they are rather than judge them by what is on the outside.

I'm eating lunch in the cafeteria, sort of bored with the regular day when Stan, who is okay but not a close friend, joins the lunch table. I open a squirt package of ketchup and accidentally/on purpose lean over and squirt it on Stan and say, "Oh… my bad." And then I start laughing – others join in the laughter.

BEHAVIOR CHANGE WORKSHEET

What bullying behavior do you feel you need to change?

- ☐ pushing, hitting
- ☐ threatening
- ☐ hurtful teasing
- ☐ name calling
- ☐ rumors, gossiping

- ☐ exclusion, eye rolling
- ☐ bossing
- ☐ controlling
- ☐ manipulating
- ☐ Other: _____

MAKE A PLAN FOR CHANGE

STEP 1: Find someone you trust to talk over what has happened and what you did wrong. Summarize the problem: What I did wrong was _____
_____.

STEP 2: Find your courage and APOLOGIZE. I will apologize to _____ and I will say: _____.
Something nice I can do for the person to make amends is: _____.

STEP 3: Imagine yourself with improved behavior. Describe the improved behavior by completing the statement: From now on I will _____
_____.

STEP 4: The New Improved You… Create a reminder for yourself to work on the improved behavior. Draw a picture of you using the improved behavior or write a reminder note. Hang the picture or note where you can see it each morning at the beginning of your day.

STEP 5: Report to someone, keep a journal of your progress, or rate yourself on a calendar. If you choose to rate yourself on the calendar use the following rating scale: Mark "3" for reaching your goal of improved behavior, mark "2" for still working, or mark "1" for back-stepping. My plan to record my progress is _____.

STEP 6: Ask a friend you trust or an adult to be your mentor/cheerleader to give you encouragement to work on the behavior goal. I will ask_____
to help with my plan.

Don't Be A Wrinkle in Someone's Heart.

Dear Parent,

In our class lesson today, we focused on reviewing our present behavior and adding or making changes so that we are showing respect for ourselves and others (working toward being kind and caring to others).

We used the visual of a "heart" as a symbol of care and love as well as the essence of life. We referred to the classic Christmas movie – Scrooge by Dickens. In the movie, Scrooge had a chance, after the visits from the three spirits (past, present, and future), to change his life to be a better person – he had a change of heart!

In the lesson, we reviewed specific behaviors – tossing the hurtful behaviors and holding on to our kind, caring behaviors. Some of the behaviors we tossed were: hitting, pushing, shoving, threatening, hurtful teasing, name-calling, excluding, eye-rolling, bossing, controlling, manipulation, and spreading rumors. Ask your son or daughter what the following statement means, "Don't be a wrinkle in someone's heart."

We personalized the lesson by asking each student to review his/her own life and the behavior choices. As the student pinpoints an area for improvement, a Behavior Change Worksheet is available to the student to guide them through the process of improving the behavior.

At home, you can reinforce this lesson by complimenting your child as he/she is caring, does a kind deed, or is thoughtful in his/her words or actions. As you see your child do unkind or hurtful behavior, address this problem. Discuss specific ways to make amends and encourage your child to have a 'change of heart'.

As always, thank you for working together. If you have any questions or concerns, please feel free to call.

Sincerely,

School Counselor

BULLY PROOF DEFENSE SHIELD

Purpose:
To review an understanding of "why" people bully and then to learn five strategies for handling it when you are a target of bullying.

Estimated Time:
30-45 minutes

Materials Needed:
Chart paper/marker or board space to make a list

Overhead transparency of the Bully Proof Defense Shield on page 98

Copy of the Bully Proof Defense Shield on page 98 for each student

Procedure:
1. On the board or chart paper write "Direct Bullying" and "Indirect Bullying". Ask for students to give examples of each type of bullying. Your list may include the following:

   Direct Bullying – hitting, pushing, punching, kicking, taunting/teasing, threatening

   Indirect Bullying – spreading rumors, gossip, exclusion, eye-rolls, manipulation, controlling

   (Explain a type of "indirect bullying" that is termed Relational Aggression or RA. Relational Aggression involves hurting someone or using aggressive behaviors within a social relationship or friendship. The purpose of relationally aggressive behaviors is to socially exclude or damage a person's reputation or status within the peer group.)

2. Next ask students to share reasons "why" they think people do "direct bullying" and then brain storm reasons why people may do "indirect bullying". Some of the reasons may be the same for both list but may include:

   Direct Bullying – to show-off for friends, bored, for power, because bullying was done to them, jealous, unable to appreciate people's differences

   Indirect Bullying- Popular girl trying to hold on to her status (fear/power), girl in the middle may join the mean girl behavior for fear of being left out or fear of being the next target, jealous.

   Point out that these reasons have nothing to do with the target personally. The target is just "used" to achieve what they need.

3. Display the "Bully Proof Defense Shield" on the overhead and handout a copy to each student. Tell the student that when they find themselves as the target in a bully situation the shield can provide some helpful information on how to deal with the problem so that they do not become a victim of bullying. Explain that the shield has some missing information that we need to review and complete together.

4. Focus on section 1 of the shield – perhaps on the overhead cover the other areas so that only section 1 is visible. Ask a student to read the sentence in section 1. Ask if the statement is 'true' or 'false'. Follow up with confirming that the statement "Just because someone called me a name or said something mean doesn't make it true" is a "true" statement. Ask a volunteer to explain why.

5. Focus on section 2 of the shield. Ask a student to read the sentence in this section. Ask for thoughts on what it means. Allow time for the students to complete the blanks by adding information about themselves on what they are good, their good qualities, and something they have done recently that they are proud of.

6. Focus on section 3 of the shield. Explain the idea of a thought bubble as what we tell ourselves – what we are thinking in our heads. Term this as "Self Talk". Share with the students that when we are in a difficult situation it is important to combat it with positive self-talk or thoughts. Give examples of positive self-talk statements and ask for students to create additional statements. Write these on the board or newsprint. Examples may include:
   ❋ I can stay calm.
   ❋ I don't believe what she says.
   ❋ I'm more mature than they are.
   ❋ I am not like that.

   Next, allow the students to copy one or several statements in their section 3 of their Bully Proof Defense Shield.

7. Focus on section 4 of the shield. Brainstorm together a list of "okay things to DO or SAY" that would help a bullying situation. Examples may include:
   ❋ Be assertive, tell the person to "Stop"
   ❋ Maintain my confidence with head high
   ❋ Make new friends
   ❋ Get involved in different activities

   Allow students time to write down suggestions on their shield.

8. Focus on section 5 of the shield. Fill in the blank with the word "Report It" so the sentence reads "Bullying is not okay, Report It." Allow time for the student to fill in their blank. Explain how conflicts are normal disagreements and they do need to handle those on their own, but that bullying is not normal and it is important to let adults know. If you have a procedure in place at your school for reporting bullying, share. Included on page 35 is a Bully Report Form, feel free to copy and make this available for your students.

Summary Poster:
Copy and display in the classroom the summary poster on p. 99. The poster is intended to be a visual reminder for the students and a tool for the teacher in reinforcing the lesson and for connecting the learning to real life situations.

Parent Letter:
Copy the parent letter on page 100 for each student to take home. The parent letter is intended to update the home on information shared so the school and home can work together to reinforce the information/skills presented.

BULLY PROOF DEFENSE SHIELD

1.

Just because someone called me a name or said something mean, doesn't make it true.

☐ TRUE   ☐ FALSE

2.

I will believe in myself. Who I am is not defined by others.

Right Turn Only →

Head in the "right" direction.

I am good at — — — — — — —

One of my good qualities is — — — — —

Recently, I am proud that I — — — — —

3. What positive self-talk is in your thought bubble?

4. **Okay things to "DO"**

_____

_____

and "SAY"

_____

_____

Bullying is NOT OKAY

_____

BULLY PROOF DEFENSE SHIELD

1.

Just because someone called me a name or said something mean, doesn't make it true.

☑ TRUE ☐ FALSE

2.

I will believe in myself. Who I am is not defined by others.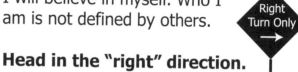

Right Turn Only →

Head in the "right" direction.

I am good at music, sports, creative writing, etc.

One of my good qualities is that I am a good listener.

Recently, I am proud that I made an "A" on my science project.

3.

What positive self-talk is in your thought bubble?

I can stay calm.
I don't have to believe what she says.
I'm more mature than they are.
I am not like that.

4. Okay things to "DO"

Maintain my confidence with head high
Make new friends
Get involved in different activities

and "SAY"

Be assertive, tell the person to "Stop"

Bullying is NOT OKAY

Report it

CLASS LESSONS

Dear Parent,

As we continue our emphasis on Bullying, our focus in our class lesson today was on learning strategies for handling it when you are a target of bullying. We reinforced the point that even though we may be a target of bullying, we can prevent ourselves from being a victim of bullying by using helpful strategies so that it does not negatively affect us.

We created a "Bully Proof Defense Shield" to help review five helpful strategies to use when we are the target of bullying. They are:

- Even though someone said it or called you a name doesn't make it true.
- It's important to value ourselves.
- Use positive self-talk to help deal.
- Recall okay things to SAY or DO to help (Remember we must find a good or okay way to deal with the problem – revenge and getting back at the person is not okay.)
- Report it – get help.

The best defense for bullying is for our sons or daughters to feel valued and confident in who they are and to respect themselves and others. It is this shield of "confidence" that will help them deal with difficult situations. Continue to reinforce for your child the specifics that make them a valued person, perhaps – a creative thinker, a person who makes good choices, enjoyable to be around, etc.

If you would like additional information on how to help your child deal when he/she is a target of bullying please feel free to call. As always, thank you for working together for our children.

Sincerely,

School Counselor

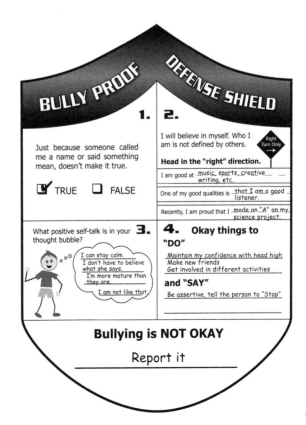

BYSTANDER – CALL TO ACTION

Purpose:
To review strategies in how the bystander can help in a bully situation.

Estimated Time:
30-45 minutes

Materials Needed:
A copy of each of the three alternate endings to the story, cut apart, ready to hand to three different students to read. See page 103.

Create a poster board of the information given on the summary poster on page 105. Cover each of the five strategies with a strip of extra poster board that can be removed/uncovered during the class discussion.

A copy of the unfinished story for each student to complete. See page 104.

Procedure:
1. Ask students what it means to play the role of the "bystander" in a bully situation. Clarify that the bystander is the one who witnesses or sees the bullying happening.

2. Ask for volunteers and hand out to three different students a different story ending. Ask that they be ready to read these out loud when called on.

3. Explain to the students that you will be reading a story about bullying; however, the story can have different endings depending on how the bystander chooses to handle the situation. Encourage the student to listen and decide if the bystander handled the bullying situation in a helpful way. Begin reading the story beginning then ask your first student to read their ending. Discuss if this was a helpful way to handle the situation – will it help stop the bullying. Review part of the story beginning again, but call on the second student to read their ending. Discuss if this was a helpful way to help with bullying. Continue on with reviewing the story beginning, but call on the third student to read their ending – then discuss.

4. Summarize that none of those strategies was an appropriate way to help in a bullying situation however we may have all seen ourselves in that situation before. Share that, across the United States, a poll was taken of effective ways for a Bystander to handle/help in a bully situation and the top five answers are on this poster board. Display the poster with the answers covered. Challenge the students to guess the top five. As students give their suggestions you may choose to turn to the poster and say, "And the answer is... not listed on the top five." Or "And the answer is...#3 "Invite the target to join your group." Uncover the answer as you read it. Continue until all answers are uncovered and discussed.

5. Distribute to each student the unfinished bystander story and ask each to write their own creative ending of the bystander story using a helpful way to handle the bullying situation. Students may refer to the displayed poster. After allowing time for the student to complete their story, encourage students to read/share their story with the class. You may choose to display these stories.

Summary Poster:

Copy and display in the classroom the summary poster on p. 105. The poster is intended to be a visual reminder for the students and a tool for the teacher in reinforcing the lesson and for connecting the learning to real life situations.

Parent Letter:

Copy the parent letter on page 106 for each student to take home. The parent letter is intended to update the home on information shared so the school and home can work together to reinforce the information/skills presented.

BYSTANDER STORY:
What Should I do?

STORY BEGINNING:

It had been a boring class in Math today. Mrs. Randolph gave us nothing but seat-work to do to review our work. When the bell rang, I was ready to be out of there. I walked up to two of my close friends, Natalie and Shayna, in the hallway at their lockers. As I got there, I realized they were making fun of Samantha, whose locker was next to theirs. They were saying, "Where did you get that outfit of yours – it is totally out of style. And those shoes look like they came from the Salvation Army!" They began laughing as I saw Samantha's face turn red and her eyes go to the floor.

FIRST STORY ENDING

Even though Samantha is not a close friend, we do have English class together and she has always seemed nice. I felt bad for Samantha – what Natalie and Shayna were doing was wrong. I feel caught… what they are doing is wrong but they are my best friends and I'm scared to say anything for fear they may turn on me and use me as the target of their laughter. I'll just be quiet and hope it will go away.

SECOND STORY ENDING

People are always making fun of others and hurting feelings. I'm so use to it happening, I just ignore it and keep going. Picking on people is normal.

THIRD STORY ENDING

I joined in and made fun of Samantha and laughed with Natalie and Shayna. After all, they are my best friends and I have to follow Natalie's led so I will fit in with their group. I wouldn't want them to think I'm not one of them!

BYSTANDER STORY: What Should I do?

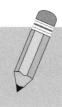

It had been a boring class in Math today. Mrs. Randolph gave us nothing but seat-work to do to review our work. When the bell rang, I was ready to be out of there. I walked up to two of my close friends, Natalie and Shayna, in the hallway at their lockers. As I got there, I realized they were making fun of Samantha, whose locker was next to theirs. They were saying, "Where did you get that outfit of yours – it is totally out of style. And those shoes look like they came from the Salvation Army!" They began laughing as I saw Samantha's face turn red and her eyes go to the floor.

_____

_____

_____

_____

_____

_____

_____

_____

_____

_____

_____

TOP 5 WAYS
FOR A BYSTANDER
TO EFFECTIVELY HANDLE
A BULLY SITUATION

Refuse to watch.

If you have equal power - ask the bully to "stop", or you can distract, or change the subject.

Invite the target to join your group.

Support the target, write a note or tell him/her that you don't agree with the bully.

Report it.

Dear Parent,

Today's lesson focused on the role of the bystander in a bullying situation. The bystander is defined as the person who witnesses or sees the bullying happening. It is the bystander who has great power to make a difference in the bullying situation. The bystander can no longer:

* do nothing for fear it may happen to them because it IS happening to someone else;

* take an "I don't care, don't want to get involved attitude and ignore" because we are a school family – a community family – a world family and we need to be there to help each other;

* Stand and watch or join in and laugh at the situation.

If we as a bystander do nothing then we are supporting the bullying behavior.

Our lesson shared the following five suggestions of ways for a bystander to help in a bully situation:
1. Refuse to watch.
2. If you have equal power - ask the bully to "stop", or you can distract, or change the subject.
3. Invite the target to join your group.
4. Support the target, write a note or tell him/her that you don't agree with the bully.
5. Report it.

As parents, we can role model for our children the importance of making a difference by getting involved to help others. As you support your child and encourage them to help others in a difficult situation, acknowledge that the choice to help others is not always easy, but the pride in knowing that you did the right thing can be priceless. Compliment your son or daughter when you see them take a stand for what is right.

As always, thank you for your support as we work together for our children. If you have any questions or concern, please feel free to ask.

Sincerely,

School Counselor

CHAPTER 3

Parent Information on Girl Bullying

Parenting can be one of the most challenging jobs. To meet that challenge, it takes an understanding of the child's world and what they deal with on a daily basis. Is there a difference between the "girls world" and the "boys world"? The majority would respond emphatically "YES!" giving supporting statements such as, "With guys you know where you stand, but girls are secretive and manipulative; they target you where they know you're the weakest. They are two-faced and can destroy you from the inside. I feel a lot safer with guys."

To be able to help and guide our daughters through those growing up years - to help them successfully maneuver through their social relationships - we need to understand their world. Girls are social beings who value the importance of fitting in and having friends. A girl's friendship group can provide comfort, closeness, and fun but can also be the source of the most pain and hurt. In girls' attempts to survive in the girl world, girls can resort to participating in rumors, gossip, hurtful teasing, bossing, controlling, betraying a friendship and more. Girls typically end up on both sides of the problem at some point – either participating in the mean or bullying behavior or being a target or victim of that behavior and at times caught in the middle.

This first part of this chapter includes a Parent Workshop: Bullying – It Happens in the Girl's World. The goal of the parent workshop is to bring parents an awareness of the girls' world, an understanding of girl bullying, how to make a positive impact to prevent the negative effects of bullying, and to share information on how to help our daughters effectively deal with the different roles of bullying – bullying behavior, target/victim, and bystander. The information shared for the parent workshop is intended for a one-hour long session.

Other information in the chapter includes Parent Handouts on girl bullying. Parent Handouts may be shared on an individual, as needed, basis, as take home information or as material to use for discussion at follow-up parent meetings. Also included in this chapter is a guideline for forming a **Parent's Book Club to further explore the topic of girl bullying.**

PARENT WORKSHOP ON GIRL BULLYING

Goal:

The goal of the parent workshop is to bring parents an awareness of the girls' world, an understanding of girl bullying, how to make a positive impact to prevent the negative effects of bullying, and to share information on how to help our daughters effectively deal with the different roles of bullying – bullying behavior, target/victim, and bystander.

Materials Needed:

Copy overhead transparencies of pages 110-122 or create a power point with the information given.

Procedure:

Show the slide information and discuss. Use the "Discussion Information" given at the bottom of each page as a guideline to guide and facilitate the discussion.

PARENT INFORMATION

PARENT WORKSHOP

BULLYING –
IT HAPPENS IN
THE GIRLS' WORLD

DISCUSSION INFORMATION:

Welcome the parents. Allow time for each parent to introduce his/her self, sharing the age/grade of their daughter and what they are hoping to gain from this workshop.

Ask the parent what they think is meant by the title, "Bullying – It Happens in the Girls' World. Summarize their answers and lead into the next slide.

UNDERSTANDING THE GIRLS' WORLD

Girls are typically social beings – with their identity gained within social groups.

- **Relational Aggression is:**

  aggressive, hurtful behaviors from within social relationships or friendship groups

  the main form of bullying used by girls (Girl Bullying)

DISCUSSION INFORMATION:

Discuss the following: Girls are typically more social oriented beings who form their identities from relationships with others. Girls value the importance of fitting in and having friends. A girl's friendships can provide closeness, comfort, and fun but can also be the source of the most pain and hurt. In attempts to survive in the girls' world they can resort to spreading rumors, gossip, hurtful teasing, controlling, manipulating, betraying a friend, and more – girl bullying.

Relational aggression or "RA" is a term coined by Dr. Nicki Crick in the early nineties and involves aggressive or hurtful behavior that is exhibited within a social relationship. The purpose of these indirect bullying behaviors is to socially exclude or damage a person's reputation or status within the peer group and can be motivated by either fear of not being a part of a group or to gain power and prestige in a desired group. The main form of girl bullying is the more covert, hidden relational aggression, however, girls can also bully openly, with aggressive, direct behavior of pushing, shoving, threatening, etc.

PARENT INFORMATION

THE ROLES WITHIN THE GIRLS' SOCIAL GROUP*

- **The Queen**
- **The Wannabee**
- **The Floater**
- **The Target**

- **The Sidekick**
- **The Gossiper**
- **The Direct Bully**
- **The Bystander**

DISCUSSION INFORMATION:

Briefly explore some of the possible roles within a friendship group:

- *The leader or the **"Queen"** is the one who has the power of the group and can resort to manipulation and control to keep the power.*
- *The **"Sidekick"** is the person who always supports the queen because that is where the power is, she allows herself to be controlled and manipulated in order to fit in.*
- *The **"Wannabee"** is the person who wants to be just like the leader enjoying the power/popularity and will go to great lengths to get the approval.*
- *The **"Gossiper"** gains her power from seeking information from others to improve her position.*
- *The **"Floater"** is the girl who moves in and out of different groups not needing a specific group for her self-esteem and identity. She does not seek power but shows respect and does not exclude other girls.*
- *The **"Direct Bully"** is the girl who uses physical violence with pushing, shoving, and threatening types of behavior.*
- *The **"Target"** is the person receiving the hurtful, mean behaviors. She can become a victim when she allows the other girls' indirect bullying and mean behaviors of exclusion, rumors, eye-rolls, hurtful teasing, etc. to negatively affect herself by feeling humiliated, exposed, and tempted to change to fit in.*
- *The **"Bystander"** is the person who witnesses the bullying or mean girl behavior and can feel caught in the middle. She may be afraid of being the next victim or afraid to go against the one with the power or not wanting to choose sides between friends.*

Caution the parent against using these labels in speaking to or in referencing their daughter's friends. Information is given more so for understanding of how complicated the girls' world can be in trying to maneuver within their social relationships.

* Information adapted with permission from the MEAN GIRLS professional seminar provided by Developmental Resources, Inc. (1-800-251-6805).

DO GIRLS BULLY DIFFERENTLY THAN BOYS?

HOW?

DISCUSSION INFORMATION:

Listen and summarize their answers.

Point out that both boys and girls can exhibit all kinds of bullying behavior - both direct (open, aggressive) and indirect (hidden, 'behind your back'). Boys typically are more direct about their bullying gaining their power with pushing, showing, and threatening. Girls, since they typically gain their identities through friendships and social relationships, are more likely to engage in indirect forms of bullying such as spreading rumors, controlling, manipulating, and exclusion — relational aggression.

Even though we may typically think that boys use the more direct, aggressive type of bullying and girls the indirect bullying, be aware that girls can be aggressive with their shoving, hitting, or "in your face" type of behavior as well as boys participating in rumors and exclusion.

PARENT INFORMATION

BULLYING IS DEFINED AS REPEATED BEHAVIORS INTENDED TO HURT SOMEONE PHYSICALLY, EMOTIONALLY, OR SOCIALLY AND USUALLY INVOLVES AN IMBALANCE OR A PERCEIVED IMBALANCE OF POWER.

DISCUSSION INFORMATION:

Share and discuss the definition of bullying. Explain that "Bullying" refers to both direct and the indirect actions (relational aggressive behavior common in girl bullying).

Explain that behaviors intended to hurt may be physical, or emotional/social like rumors, exclusion, controlling, manipulating, bossing, etc. Explain that imbalance of power might be body weight/size or it can be perceived popularity or advanced social skills. Bullying, either direct or indirect, is not okay. It is never okay to intentionally and repeatedly hurt another person.

Explain the difference between conflict and bullying. Explain that "conflict" occurs when two or more people who have equal powers have a disagreement. "Bullying" occurs when a more powerful person or group repeatedly uses that power to hurt or control another person. Conflicts are a normal part of life, bullying is not.

THREE ROLES OF A BULLY SITUATION ARE:

1. BULLY BEHAVIOR

2. TARGET/VICTIM

3. BYSTANDER

DISCUSSION INFORMATION:

Explain that the bullying situation has three roles:

1. *The behavior that is hurtful or mean is the BULLY BEHAVIOR. Explain that the person is not a 'bad person' but their choice to be mean is a bad choice. Bully behavior can include direct bully behavior of pushing, shoving, hitting, and intimidating or indirect bullying behavior (relational aggression) of controlling, manipulating, spreading rumors, bossing, and excluding.*

2. *The TARGET/VICITM is the person receiving the bullying behavior. Point out that a person can be a target without being a victim by choosing not to let the bully behavior affect them in a negative way.*

3. *Share that the BYSTANDER is the witness or person standing by seeing the problem. Bystanders have the power to make a positive difference in the situation. As a bystander you may feel scared that you may be next, or are so used to bullying behavior that you ignore, or the bystander may laugh or join in with the bullying. Share that none of these approaches are helpful. Encourage the bystander to use their power for good - to take the risk and get involved to help.*

Point out that we can typically end up in each of the three roles at different times; therefore, our goal is to give the girls skills to handle it when they find themselves in each of the roles. We will be looking at specific strategies that we as parents can use to help our daughters in the different roles.

CYBER-BULLYING

WHAT DOES THAT MEAN?
Using cyberspace (computers and cell phones) to bully others.

DANGERS of this new method of bullying:
- Only a click of a button to send hurtful messages/rumors
- Can bully day or night
- Can create websites of stories/pictures/jokes ridiculing others
- Things are said that would never be said "face to face"
- Gives a sense of anonymity – may say things because you think no one will find out.

Ways to HELP:
- Become computer knowledgeable
- Talk to your child about Cyber-bullying. Tell your child if they wouldn't say it face to face then don't type it on the computer or phone.
- Discuss Internet Safety
- Monitor your child's computer activity
- Report illegal use of on-line behavior

DISCUSSION INFORMATION:

Review the above information. You may choose to review the parent handout page 128 CYBER-BULLYING TIPS FOR PARENTS, for additional information.

WHY FOCUS ON THE ISSUE OF GIRL BULLYING?

HOW DO WE MAKE A POSITIVE IMPACT TO PREVENT GIRL BULLYING?

- **Help our children develop a strong sense of self**

- **Empathy building**

- **Good moral values**

- **Friendship skills**

- **Good communication skills**

- **Good character building – respectful, responsible, honest, cooperative, good citizen, self disciplined**

DISCUSSION INFORMATION:

Share that our goal is to encourage each girl to seek value and power in healthy, appropriate ways showing respect for herself and others. It is important to focus on the issue of bullying because our girls are rehearsing their roles now for adulthood. We would not want our daughter entering the adult world manipulating or controlling to achieve power nor would we want our daughter to enter the adult world thinking it is okay to be a victim of someone's abuse or mistreatment.

POSITIVE IMPACT – Share the following:
- *Build confidence that she is a good person. This confidence comes from within and is not dependent on outside judgments, acceptance or compliments.*
- *Discuss feelings openly to build empathy. When watching TV or reading a book together discuss the people's feelings involved, or share something that happened at work or school that creates empathy or caring about a situation.*
- *Emphasize your family values of what you value as right and wrong in relation to people.*
- *Point out examples and compliment good acts of friendship.*
- *Stress the importance of being open and honest. Teach 'I messages' to communicate when feelings are hurt. Teach the importance of getting the facts.*
- *Make a specific effort to use the character words in labeling/complimenting a behavior.*

Ask: After working on the above will it totally prevent bullying? No, but it will help reduce and prepare our daughters.

WHAT NOT TO DO?

IF YOUR CHILD IS BULLYING:

- Don't ignore.
- Don't punish but discipline instead – it's a learning process.

IF YOUR CHILD IS THE TARGET OR VICTIM:

- Don't minimize, rationalize, or explain away the bully behavior.
- Don't blame your child for doing something to aggravate the bully.
- Don't rush in to solve the problem for your child
- Don't tell your child to fight back.
- Don't rush to confront the bully or the bully's parents

IF YOUR CHILD IS THE BYSTANDER:

- Don't tell your child to not get involved.

DISCUSSION INFORMATION:

Review and discuss the above information.

Remind the parent if their child has engaged in some girl bullying to not do the guilt thing but to remember how strong peer pressure is with the need to fit in and gain social identity.

Explain that the upcoming slides will give specific information on "what to do" to help your daughter in each of the three roles of bullying.

WHAT TO DO TO HELP WHEN YOUR DAUGHTER IS USING BULLY BEHAVIOR?

- **Intervene immediately with Discipline - restitution, resolution, and reconciliation.***
- **Create opportunities to "do good" and compliment.**
- **Nurture empathy.**
- **Use the Behavior Change Worksheet.**
- **Monitor TV, computer activities, and music.**
- **Be a positive role model.**
- **Engage in more constructive, entertaining, and energizing activities.**

*adapted with permission from Barbara Colorosa (2003). The Bully, the Bullied, and the Bystander. New York, NY: HarpersCollins Publishers Inc.

DISCUSSION INFORMATION:

- *Point out the importance to focus not on punishment but on discipline – to respectfully provide learning through consequences. Explain that restitution involves fixing what you did wrong – apologize, tell others involved you were wrong, etc. Resolution involves figuring out how you will keep it from happening again. And reconciliation is to come up with a way to heal the hurt – perhaps by inviting the other person to participate in a friend activity.*

- *Encourage your child to show care and concern for others by helping a brother/sister with schoolwork he/she is having trouble with or helping a neighbor or help at a church activity.*

- *Spend time talking about your feelings and the feelings of others.*

- *Share/handout the Behavior Change Worksheet on page 93.*

- *Supervise and limit TV, computer, and music.*

- *Review our own behavior – actions speak louder than words. Make a point to share.*

- *Engage in positive gossips at the dinner table.*

- *Find fun, creative, and healthy activities to participate in - a better use of our time.*

WHAT TO DO TO HELP WHEN YOUR DAUGHTER IS THE TARGET OR VICTIM?

- Be a good listener.

- Let your child know that she is not alone in this.

- Let her know that it is not her fault.

- Compliment her on her ability to share this problem and compliment her strengths – empower.

- Guide her through the problem-solving process.

- Role-play ways to handle and be assertive.

- Involve your child in activities outside of school.

- Be a positive role model.

DISCUSSION INFORMATION:

Review and discuss the above information

You may choose to refer to the PROBLEM-SOLVING MODEL WORKSHEET on page 207 to use to guide her through the problem-solving process.

WHAT TO DO TO HELP WHEN YOUR DAUGHTER IS A BYSTANDER?

- Help your child eliminate excuses for not getting involved.
- Review different ways to help:
    - Refuse to join in on the hurtful behavior.
    - Change the subject.
    - Tell the person doing the bullying to stop.
    - Be a friend to the target/victim.
    - Tell an adult.
- Compliment your child when she has helped a friend in a difficult situation.
- Be a positive role model.

DISCUSSION INFORMATION:

Explain that excuses such as "The bully is my friend..." or "She's a loser anyway." or "It's not my problem! This is not my fight!" are not okay excuses. The bystander has the power to make a positive difference.

Explain that the bystander can tell the person doing the bullying to stop. This option is effective if they feel the person doing the bullying would listen. If not, explain that you the bystander can help the target by inviting her to join their group or by letting her know later that you overheard what was said and that you don't agree with the mean words. If the target continues to be a victim of the mean words and behavior, then involving a helpful adult is important.

Emphasize the importance of complimenting and supporting your daughter as she works to help a friend.

Share that actions speak louder than words, so it's important to help others. When you have helped someone out, talk with your daughter about 'what' and 'why' you helped.

PARENT INFORMATION

WHAT IS SOMETHING DIFFERENT YOU LEARNED ABOUT THE GIRLS' WORLD AND BULLYING?

Think of three new specific things you want to do to make a positive difference for your daughter.

"Success is to be measured not so much by the position that one has reached in life as by the obstacles one has overcome while trying to succeed."

— by Booker T. Washington

DISCUSSION INFORMATION:

Listen, clarify, and summarize information shared.

Ask each parent to make a commitment to try three new strategies that can help.

Review the quote. Point out that this quote can have meaning not only for our daughters as they seek success but also for us as parents as we know that our success as parents only comes through hard work and overcoming obstacles and difficulties in parenting.

PARENT INFORMATION

Understanding Girl Bullying

Girls can bully openly and directly by hitting, pushing, or threatening, but typically, girls bully more indirectly and discreetly by spreading rumors, excluding, eye rolling, and sending hurtful messages. This type of bullying can be just as harmful if not more harmful than physical bullying. Girls gain their identity within the social context and their role with their peers; therefore, it is often within this social context that girls hurt each other by social exclusion or damaging a person's reputation or status in the peer group. This type of indirect bullying is termed "relational aggression".

Bullying involves three roles: the bully behavior, the target/victim, and the bystander. The **bully behavior** is the person who is repeatedly aggressing or using harmful behaviors with the intention of hurting. I use the term bully behavior as opposed to "bully" to reduce the implication that the "bully" is a bad person, instead she has made a bad choice in her behavior. In the role of the **target/victim** we need to realize that yes, we more than likely will end up a target of cruel behavior at some point but that by choosing to handle it in a positive way and not letting the cruel behavior bother us we are preventing ourselves from becoming a victim of bullying. The role of the **bystander** has a great deal of power to make a difference in our school, community, and world by taking a stand to help and care for others.

As we explore the issue of girl bullying we realize that girls can easily go in and out of all three roles - being a target/victim in one situation and then a bully in another. We need to identify these roles, understand them, recognize our behavior in the roles, and then make good choices to handle the role in an appropriate way whether it be a change from the bully behavior, building confidence to not allow yourself to be a victim, or moving to action as a bystander to help make a difference.

It is important to help our children care about others, to be kind to our siblings and peers, to share, get along with others, and make and sustain friendships. Helping our children develop these skills will go a long way in counteracting the temptation to join the social pressures to participate in bullying behavior.

Parent Suggestions to Help Prevent/Prepare for Girl Bullying:

* **Spend time with your child.** Have a special time together either at meal time or bed time to talk and be there for her. Watch TV together – even her shows for an opportunity to understand her world.

* **Be consistent about discipline.** Hold your child responsible for negative or hurtful behavior, not through put-downs or punishment but through her understanding the consequences of her actions.

* **Know your child's friends.** Chaperone trips, provide transportation for your daughter and her friends, and allow kids to gather at your home.

✳ **Help your child see other points of view and develop empathy for others.**
Take time to ask:
"Who did you help today?" When watching a TV show or movie that involves bullying and relationships, explore the different roles and perspectives.

✳ **Be a positive role model.** Actions speak louder than words. Try positive gossips at the dinner table – looking for the good in people.

A Word About Bullying Among Siblings:

Some degree of conflict among siblings is expected; however, sibling rivalry can develop into bullying as children compete for power. We want our children to learn to work out their conflicts and disagreements themselves in an appropriate, healthy way using their problem solving skills. In a conflict, both sides have equal power to resolve the problem; however, bullying involves the intentional, one-sided use of power to control another. So...at what point do we get involved? Generally, behavior that would be unacceptable between two unrelated children is unacceptable between two siblings. When one child intentionally and consistently hurts a less powerful sibling – that's bullying. Family involvement in stopping bullying is important.

WHEN MY DAUGHTER HAS <u>BULLYING BEHAVIORS</u>:
How to Help

Barbara Coloroso, in her book *The Bully, the Bullied, and the Bystander*, summarizes seven helpful things to do to help:

1. When a child does something wrong, intervene immediately with discipline not punishment. Discipline involves the child taking ownership of the problem (no excuses) and the child solving the problem or 'fixing' the problem through restitution, resolution, or reconciliation. Restitution involves "fixing" what she did – replacing item, apologizing, etc. Resolution means to figure out a way to keep the incident from happening again – what can she change about her behavior. Reconciliation is a process of healing with the person and can involve extending the hand of friendship to participate in a fun activity together or to help the other person with something.

2. Create opportunities to "do good". Provide opportunities for her to help a neighbor with yard work or a brother/sister with homework , or volunteer at a church activity.

3. Nurture empathy. It is important to be able to look at others' perspectives and to understand their feelings. This can be done by "putting ourselves in their place", processing their nonverbal and verbal cues and understanding their life experiences. This skill can be developed by asking questions on how you think someone might be feeling and why – discuss how to respond to help them, or use a TV show to discuss the feelings.

4. Teach friendship skills. It is important to help our child learn to be assertive, respectful, and to relate to others in peaceful ways. A discussion about friendship can be prompted with the saying, "To have a friend, you must first be a friend." Ask you daughter what she values in a friend, make a list, and then encourage her to be living up to her list in being a good friend to others.

5. Closely monitor TV, computer activities, and music. Be aware of all of the influences in our society for some may not be in agreement with our value system. In addition, too much media involvement and too little "real life" social interaction and engagement stifle the development of social skills necessary to relate in a caring, responsible way.

6. Engage in more constructive, entertaining, and energizing activities. Needs can be met in a more healthy, appropriate way of a fun activity rather than the hurt of bullying someone.

7. Teach your child to "will good". Encouraging our children to have moral integrity to do what is right even in difficult situations.

WHEN MY DAUGHTER IS A <u>TARGET/VICTIM</u> OF BULLYING:
How to Help

Parenting is always a challenge. When our children are upset our emotions seem to auto-matically "kick-in"; therefore, it is important to, first, calm down and be in control of your own emotions. Caution yourself not to let your own personal bullying experiences from your past influence your ability to help. Be careful that you don't take over to try to 'solve' the problem, this sends the message that she is not strong enough to handle the situation on her own and be careful that you don't send a blaming message asking, "What did you do wrong? What are you doing to cause this?" This can add to her fear of low self worth. The following provides some strategies for parents to support their child when she is upset:

❋ Be a good listener. Listen without the distraction of the computer, newspaper, phone etc.

❋ Ask questions that invite more information such as, "What happened next?" or "What did you do?"

❋ Listen to the whole story encouraging her to share details. Allowing your child to talk in details to vent and get out the story can be therapeutic.

❋ Repeat back what you are hearing your daughter share. This can help clarify the situation. Ex. "So you're saying that the girls wouldn't allow you to sit with them and they told you do not ever sit with them again."

❋ Give a hug – hold her.

❋ Don't over-empathize – empower her. Compliment her on her abilities. Ex. "I know that this is hard. You're amazing to be able to express yourself about this."

❋ Ask if she can think of something to say or do that would be helpful. Encourage assertiveness. Role-play for practice. Help her rehearse the messages in her head to build confidence.

When an isolated incident occurs, show your daughter support and encourage her to figure out her own solutions. If the behavior occurs a second or third time, she needs to be encouraged to act on her own behalf. When bullying persists or is extreme, it's time to inter-vene. Don't take action behind her back, if you're going to make contact with the school, make sure she knows ahead of time.

ADDITIONAL INFORMATION FOR
Helping Your Child...

KNOW THE DIFFERENCE BETWEEN TEASING AND TAUNTING:

So often a child's response when you correct her for hurting someone's feelings is the excuse, "I was just teasing." or "Can't they take a joke?" The response makes it difficult to follow up with a correction unless we take time to clarify for our child the difference between normal teasing and hurtful teasing. In this information, we will use the word "teasing" for the intended to be fun, normal behavior and the word "taunting" for when the teasing is no longer fun but becomes harmful and hurtful.

Teasing:
✳ is intended to get both parties to laugh.
✳ pokes fun in a lighthearted clever way and is never intended to hurt.
✳ is innocent in motive.
✳ is discontinued when the person being teased becomes upsets or objects to the teasing.

Taunting:
✳ is based on an imbalance of power, is one sided and is intended to hurt or harm.
✳ involves humiliating, cruel, or demeaning comments hidden under the guise of joking.
✳ includes laughter directed at the target, not with the target.
✳ continues even though the person objects.

Taunting is not acceptable and is a form of bullying in which the person is attempting to belittle and demean another person.

RUMORS: HOW TO RECOGNIZE AND NOT PARTICPATE

Part of being friends is talking, sharing, and catching up on the news...however, so often friendship relations can lead to talking about others in a negative way and passing on rumors. It is very tempting for our child to participate in this activity but we need to take the opportunity to talk with our daughter about the damage that rumors can cause. It is important to know the difference between things that are okay and not okay to be shared or repeated. The following questions may help decide if it is okay to pass on the information: Is it true? Is it kind? If the answer is "no" to either question – don't repeat it.

HANDOUT FOR PARENTS

PARENT INFORMATION

CYBERBULLYING TIPS FOR PARENTS

The Center for Safe and Responsible Internet Use defines Cyber-Bullying as "using the internet or other mobile devices to send or post harmful or cruel text or images to bully others." The internet, instant messaging on computers, text messaging from phones are all tremendous advances in technology that bring great benefits but also open up a whole new avenue for bullying. It is important to be aware of how these can be used for bullying. The following gives some examples:

* Sending hurtful messages or rumors with a click of a key
* Creating websites that have stories, pictures, and jokes ridiculing others
* Posting pictures of classmates online and asking students to rate them
* Engaging someone in instant messaging, tricking the person into revealing sensitive information and forwarding it to others, or using three-way calling in which a person may lead the other into saying something mean about a third person who is also on the line.
* Taking a picture of a person in the locker room using a camera phone; then, sending that picture to others.

Being aware that this is our new reality, we need to be prepared as parents to educate our children as to the appropriate use of technology, to monitor the use, and to intervene if necessary.

The following list some suggestions to combat cyber-bullying:

* Become computer knowledgeable, educate yourself on the terminology and how to navigate a computer so you can speak the same language as your child.
* Do not allow your child to have a computer in their room or other isolated area. Computers need to be placed in an area that easily allows you to monitor your child's activity on the computer and the time that is being spent on the computer.
* Have a discussion about Internet safety – how the internet can be helpful and when it can be dangerous. Review safety rules for internet usage.
* Talk to your child about cyber-bullying. Ask your child if she understands what cyber-bullying is and if she has ever been cyber-bullied or has participated in writing or forwarding hurtful messages to others.
* Inquire about filtering and parental control programs to install on your computer – decide if it is right for you. However, do not rely on them for your only protection against cyber-bullying or other predators.

The following are possible websites that translate text messages and help you define those "techno" terms: www.transl8it.com and www.whatis.com used by your child.

PARENT BOOK CLUB

Purpose:
To provide a avenue for discussion and learning on the topic of Girl Bullying through the use of books.

Materials Needed:
Each participant needs a copy of the selected book.

Procedure:
Gain the participants' commitment to read the book assignments outside of the group meetings and then to meet and discuss. Provide a schedule of meetings correlated to the reading assignments.

Specific discussion questions need to be developed depending on the selected book, however, some general questions to process/discuss the reading assignments are:

1. What part of the reading did you most relate to and why?
2. Was there a part you disagreed with?
3. How can you relate this to "real life"?

Suggested Books on Girl Bullying are:

* *Girl Wars* by Cheryl Dellasega and Charisse Nixon

* *Odd Girl Out* by Rachel Simmons

* *Mean Chicks, Cliques, and Dirty Tricks* by Erika Karres

* *Queen Bees and Wannabes* by Rosalind Wiseman

* *The Bully, Bullied, and the Bystander* by Barbara Coloroso

* *Please Stop Laughing at Me…* by Jodee Blanco

* *See Jane Hit* by James Garbarino

CHAPTER 4

Small Group Counseling Sessions on Girl Bullying

SMALL GROUP COUNSELING SESSIONS TOPIC:

Surviving and Thriving in the <u>Girl World</u>

Surviving and thriving in the Girl World can be a challenge at times. Girls are social beings who value the importance of fitting in and having friends. A girl's friendship group can provide comfort, closeness, and fun but can also be the source of the most pain and hurt. In girls' attempts to survive in the girl world, girls can resort to participating in rumors, gossip, hurtful teasing, bossing, controlling, betraying a friendship, and more. This type of bullying or hurtful behavior is known as relational aggression. Relational Aggression is aggressive or hurtful behavior that is intended to hurt or harm someone by damaging or manipulating his or her relationships with others. Girls typically end up on both sides of the problem at some point – either participating in the bullying or aggressive behavior or being a target or victim of that behavior and at times caught in the middle.

Our goal of this small group experience is to provide the girls an awareness of the different roles we can play – aggressor (bully behavior), victim, and bystander. An awareness offers understanding to the victim that they are not alone, a chance for the aggressor to reevaluate her actions, and support for the bystander to take action in helping others. Specific friendship behaviors are explored in sessions 2-6 with an emphasis on "if you're guilty of the behavior, then change" and "if you are a victim of the behavior, then handle it". Remember that girls can end up on both sides of the problem at some point, therefore, it's important to explore both sides and give skills to help. The group experience will also provide an opportunity to review our own friendship style and make adjustments, to appreciate the positives about friendships, and to acknowledge the importance of valuing our true self.

Session 1 provides an introduction to the Girl World and includes a pre-assessment for the student and an optional pre-assessment for the parent/teacher in order to gain more information of the specific needs of the group. From these assessments, effective lessons can be provided. You may need to consider combining lessons, omitting lessons, and spending additional time if needed on a concept (perhaps even pulling some activities from the Individual Counseling chapter if more information is needed). I encourage you to change any examples or situations that may be more effective for your specific age group to relate. A Small Group Roster and Planning Form is given in Lesson 1 to organize the lessons and record notes and observations. Sessions 2-6 focus on specific friendship behaviors. Session 7 explores the situation of "being caught in the middle" between friends. Session 8-10 empowers each girl to value their true self, use their skills to manage conflicts, and to focus on the joy of friends.

The composition of the group should not be formed to deal with a specific problem (handle that individually) but instead to deal with general ins and outs of relationship problems. It is helpful to gain information through observation, staff members, and information shared of the typical behaviors and friendship patterns of the girls but be careful not to label any of the girls as the "aggressor", "victim", or "bystander". It is found that typically we all have been aggressors, victims, and bystanders at different times, so our energies should focus on finding healthy ways to survive and move on from these behaviors.

A parent permission letter is included in this section as well as a general teacher letter on what will be offered in the group. If additional information needs to be shared with parents, see the parent section of this book.

After the small group is concluded, follow-up is important. Remind them of discussions of the group and skills learned. Help the student apply their new skills to day to day life. Continue with individual counseling if needed – see the individual counseling chapter of this book for more information.

TEACHER RECOMMENDATON
for Small Group Counseling

To: Teachers

From:

Re: Small Group Counseling

Date:

Small group counseling is offered to students to support and enhance the development of personal and social skills and to support and promote educational success. Small groups provide not only additional social-emotional learning experiences but also allows the students a chance to belong, a chance to express themselves, and a chance to benefit from the support of group members.

At this time, small group counseling entitled "Surviving and Thriving in the Girl World" will be offered. The group will focus on the ins and outs of the girl world – how girls place importance on social relations and friends and yet how girls can hurt each other (hurtful teasing, gossiping, exclusion, controlling, bossing, betrayal) through these friendships. We will explore how to deal with the "hurt" or bullying from other girls, to assess and make adjustments in our own friendship style, to appreciate the positives about friendships, and to acknowledge the importance of valuing our true self.

If you feel that this group would meet the needs of some of your girls. Please complete the form below to submit their name with a brief description of the concern, or reason for referral

Thank you.

Small Group Topic: **SURVIVING AND THRIVING IN THE GIRL WORLD**

Referring Teacher: _____

Student's Name	Reason for Referral
_____	_____
_____	_____
_____	_____
_____	_____

Small Group Counseling

Dear Parent,

Our School Counseling Program at _____ offers small group counseling for our students. Small groups provide not only the opportunity for additional learning experiences but also a time of sharing and a time of growing together with fellow students. Small groups give the students a chance to belong, a chance to express themselves, and a chance to benefit from the support of group members.

Your daughter is invited to be a part of a small group entitled:

SURVIVING AND THRIVING IN THE GIRL WORLD

The group will focus on the ins and outs of the girl world – how girls place importance on social relations and friends and yet how girls can hurt each other (hurtful teasing, gossiping, exclusion, controlling, bossing, backstabbing) through these friendships. We will explore how to deal with the "hurt" or bullying from other girls, to assess and make adjustments in our own friendship style, to appreciate the positives about friendships, and to acknowledge the importance of valuing our true self.

The group will meet _____ during the school day.

Parent permission is requested for a student to participate in the group. Please return the bottom portion of this letter to your daughter's teacher. I will be happy to answer any questions you might have. You may reach me by calling the school.

Sincerely,

Your School Counselor

....

Permission for small group counseling

Date: _____

I agree that my daughter, _____ may participate in small group

counseling on the topic of: SURVIVING AND THRIVING IN THE GIRL WORLD.

Parent Signature: _____

SESSION 1	INSIDE THE GIRL WORLD

Purpose:

To establish the guidelines of the group meetings; to gain an overview of the ins and outs of the girls world (how friends help and how they hurt); and to complete a pre-assessment survey of friendship qualities.

Materials Needed:

Copy of the Group Guidelines on page 137

Pencils and copies of the pre-assessment survey for each participant

A bowl with a lid to resemble "The World"

Situations on page 138 cut apart and placed inside the bowl (World).

Copy of the Small Group Roster and Planning on pages 142-143

Procedure:

1. **Welcome** the girls to the group experience giving an overview of the group, sharing brief introductions, and explaining the meeting schedule.

2. Display the copy of the **group guidelines and review**. Gain a commitment from each to follow the guidelines.

3. **Place the bowl** resembling the world in front of the group. Tell the group that this is representing the "Girl World". Ask: What do we mean by GIRL WORLD? As you repeat and summarize their answers include the points that:

   ✳ girls typically want to belong, fit in, and be apart of a group

   ✳ girls are social beings who place importance on their role in being apart of a group

   ✳ it is from within that social/friendship group that we get hurt at times from gossips, exclusions, teasing, bossing, controlling, etc.

   ✳ friendships can vary from best friends to worst enemies

4. **Hand out the Student Pre-Assessment,** instructing the student to add their name and date. Explain the rating scale of 4-1 as Strongly Agree to Strongly Disagree. Read #1 and ask the girls to mark their answer by circling the number. Next, lift the lid of the bowl and say, "Let's look inside the Girl World." Have a student select or you select a slip of paper from the bowl and

read to the group. Ask the students to label the good friendship quality described in the situation - discuss. Then ask the student to locate the number on their assessment that correlates to the slip of paper selected (some numbers have an a. and b. part – both need to be marked). Remind the students to be honest as they mark. Explain that this information will be used to help plan what to focus on in the other sessions. Continue selecting slips from the bowl, reading and discussing and then each girl marking to rate herself on the pre-assessment survey. Allow time to complete question 11 and then collect the completed forms.

5. End the group session by asking each girl to **share** one thing that is good about being a girl?

Option: Tell the student that you have a similar assessment for their parent and/or teacher to complete. Explain that the information from others can give us insights as to our friendship qualities that are strong and areas that we can improve on. Either give the copies to the students to give to their teachers and parents or you may choose to put the assessment in the teachers' boxes and mail to parents. As the results come in review all the assessments on each student to determine the emphasis of the group sessions. At some point, you may choose to share the assessments with individuals in order to point out how their teacher or parent sees a friendship strength that they haven't appreciated or perhaps to gently confront on how others may see them.

Group Planning: As you review the pre-assessments, pinpoint which areas need more focus. The ten sessions provided in this chapter correlate directly with the number on the pre-assessment. Choose which lessons you plan to incorporate in the group. If additional information needs to be covered on a particular topic, review the activities in the individual counseling chapter. With some adjustments, the activities can be used in a group setting.

A **SMALL GROUP ROSTER AND PLANNING** form is included. This roster provides a place for the listing of group members, their attendance and related needs, along with plans for group sessions. Remember to use the information gathered from the needs assessments to select and determine the lessons for each session. A "note/observation" section is included on this form to record any details or specifics that arise during the session that need to be remembered or that needs to be addressed at the next session.

Group Guidelines:

✳ Treat others RESPECTFULLY.

✳ Listen to each other.

✳ Take turns in sharing.

✳ If something bothers you, confront the problem respectfully.

✳ Personal stories shared in the room, stay in the room.

✳ When sharing personal stories, don't use names of people who are not present in the group.

FRIENDSHIP SITUATIONS
IN THE GIRL WORLD

Directions:
Copy and cut apart each of the friendship situations and place in the Girl World bowl. Take turns drawing each of the slips - reading and discussing. Direct the student to find the number on the Student Pre-Assessment sheet that correlates to the number on the slip and ask the student to honestly mark their answer.

2 I usually sit with a group of my friends at lunch. When I went to sit at the table today, Lyn rolled her eyes and turned her back at me. I saw the other girls follow her lead, they saw what happened but then turned and went back to talking with other friends. It hurt, I walked away.

3 Julie came rushing up to our group and announced that she has some juicy gossip about Samantha. She said, "Do you want to hear?" I said, "I'm sorry, I don't have time, I've got to the bathroom before my next class."

4 Holly is always making cutting remarks about how I dress and then laughing. It hurts.

5 Ericka is always bossing me around and telling me what I should or should not do. I'm tired of it.

6 It really bothered me when my best friend Amy started flirting with this boy that she knew I really liked. I thought, "I'll show her, I'll tell one of her personal secrets. Then she'll know what it's like to get your feelings hurt."

7 One of my friends, Kelsey, was being teased and humiliated by my good friend Elizabeth. I felt for Kelsey, but I was afraid to say something about it to Elizabeth for fear she might turn on me.

8 I feel that I am a good person and I value who I am. I'm not going to do something wrong or hurtful just to fit in with a certain group.

9 Conflicts and disagreements can be a part of every day. I know how to communicate with my friends about the problem and to find good ways to handle it.

10 I know how to be a good friend to others.

STUDENT PRE-ASSESSMENT
for SURVIVING AND THRIVING IN THE GIRL WORLD

Student Name: _____ Date: _____

Directions: Complete the needs assessment to reflect your present behavior.
Mark your answers honestly.

		4 strongly agree	3 agree	2 disagree	1 strongly disagree
1.	I understand what is meant by being in the "Girl World".	☐	☐	☐	☐
2a.	I appreciate and include others rather than leaving others out or excluding them.	☐	☐	☐	☐
2b.	I know how to handle it when others leave me out.	☐	☐	☐	☐
3a.	I only say nice things about others and I resist the temptation to spread rumors and gossip.	☐	☐	☐	☐
3b.	I know how to handle it when others spread rumors and gossip about me.	☐	☐	☐	☐
4a.	I enjoy talking in a caring way with others rather than teasing and making fun of people.	☐	☐	☐	☐
4b.	I know how to handle it when people tease and make fun of me.	☐	☐	☐	☐
5a.	I show respect and empathy for others and do not boss or take advantage of people.	☐	☐	☐	☐
5b.	I know how to handle it when others boss or try to take advantage of me.	☐	☐	☐	☐
6a.	I am loyal and honest with others and do not betray or talk bad about people behind their back.	☐	☐	☐	☐
6b.	I know how to handle it if others betray me or talk bad about me behind my back.	☐	☐	☐	☐
7.	I know how to handle it if I am "caught in the middle" between friends.	☐	☐	☐	☐
8.	I like myself, I am a good person, and I value who I am.	☐	☐	☐	☐
9.	I know how to handle conflicts or disagreements, in helpful ways.	☐	☐	☐	☐
10.	I know how to be a good friend to others.	☐	☐	☐	☐

11. What I hope to learn from this group is: _____

_____

Dear Teacher/Parent,

Surviving and thriving in the Girl World can be a challenge at times. Girls are social beings who value the importance of fitting in and having friends. The friendship group that can provide comfort, closeness, and fun but can also be the source of the most pain and hurt. In girls attempts to survive in the girl world, girls can resort to participating in rumors, gossip, teasing, bossing, controlling, betraying a friendship, and more. Girls typically end up on both sides of the problem at some point – either participating in the mean or bullying behavior or being a target or victim of that behavior and at times caught in the middle.

In order to structure our small group experience to meet the specific needs of the group members, I need your input. Please take some time to review the child's behavior over the past months, complete the assessment survey and return. Please feel free to add comments or to share any information that would be helpful as we begin our small group experience. Thank you for your input as we work together to help our students maneuver in a helpful, positive way within the Girl World of friendships and relationships.

Sincerely,

Your School Counselor

PARENT/TEACHER PRE ASSESSMENT *for* SURVIVING AND THRIVING IN THE GIRL WORLD GROUP

Student Name: _____ Date: _____

		4 strongly agree	**3** agree	**2** disagree	**1** strongly disagree
1.	She understands what is meant by being in the "Girl World".	❒	❒	❒	❒
2a.	She appreciates and includes others rather than leaving others out or excluding them.	❒	❒	❒	❒
2b.	She knows how to handle it when others leave her out.	❒	❒	❒	❒
3a.	She only says nice things about others and she resists the temptation to spread rumors and gossip.	❒	❒	❒	❒
3b.	She knows how to handle it when others spread rumors and gossip about her.	❒	❒	❒	❒
4a.	She enjoys talking in a caring way with others rather than teasing and making fun of people.	❒	❒	❒	❒
4b.	She knows how to handle it when others tease and make fun of her.	❒	❒	❒	❒
5a.	She shows respect and empathy for others and does not boss or take advantage of people.	❒	❒	❒	❒
5b.	She knows how to handle it when others boss or tries to take advantage of her.	❒	❒	❒	❒
6a.	She is loyal and honest with others and does not betray or talk bad about people behind their back.	❒	❒	❒	❒
6b.	She knows how to handle it when others betray her.	❒	❒	❒	❒
7.	She knows how to handle it if she is "caught in the middle" between friends.	❒	❒	❒	❒
8.	She likes herself, she is a good person, and she values who she is.	❒	❒	❒	❒
9.	She knows how to handle conflicts or disagreements in helpful ways.	❒	❒	❒	❒
10.	She knows how to be a good friend to others.	❒	❒	❒	❒

Comments: _____

_____

Small Group Roster And Planning

Group Topic: _____

Student Name	Teacher	Sessions								Related Needs
		1	2	3	4	5	6	7	8	

SESSION 1:

Plans: _____
_____
_____
_____

Observations/Notes: _____
_____
_____

SESSION 2:

Plans: _____
_____
_____
_____

Observations/Notes: _____
_____
_____

SESSION 3:

Plans: _____
_____
_____
_____

Observations/Notes: _____
_____
_____

SESSION 4:

Plans: _____

_____

_____

_____

Observations/Notes: _____

_____

_____

SESSION 5:

Plans: _____

_____

_____

_____

Observations/Notes: _____

_____

_____

SESSION 6:

Plans: _____

_____

_____

_____

Observations/Notes: _____

_____

_____

SESSION 7:

Plans: _____

_____

_____

_____

Observations/Notes: _____

_____

_____

PLAN FOR FOLLOW-UP: (Complete the Student and Teacher / Parent Post Assessment and review to determine successes and area of remaining weaknesses.) _____

_____

_____

_____

_____

SESSION 2 | # EXCLUDING OTHERS vs. APPRECIATING AND INCLUDING OTHERS

Purpose:

To emphasize the importance of appreciating and valuing others as individuals. Strategies for changing the hurtful behavior of exclusion as well as dealing when you are the victim of exclusion will be discussed.

Materials Needed:

On a poster board strip write "Seek popularity not based on power, but popularity based on admirable qualities."

Marker/chart paper or poster board labeled "Admirable Qualities". (The completed chart paper or poster will be used in subsequent sessions.)

Copy, cut out, and assemble the "What To Do Cube" on page 147. (Use cardstock of available)

Copy for each student the QF (Quick Fix) Summary Sheet on page 148.

Procedure:

1. **Ask:** What does it mean to be popular?

2. **Display the poster strip** and ask them what it means to "seek popularity not based on power but popularity based on admirable qualities".

3. **Brainstorm a list of admirable qualities** and write these on the chart paper or poster board.

4. **Read aloud the story,** "Saved by the Bell". Ask the girls to determine whether the qualities of the person in the story are admirable or not. Summarize the negative attitude of "I'm better than others" that resulted in excluding behavior that was evident in the story. Discuss.

5. **Ask:** What is the opposite of "excluding others"? Illicit the answer of "including others". Further discuss that appreciating and valuing others produces the positive behavior of including other people in your group or activity. **To the "Admirable Qualities" list,** add "including others" and "appreciating and valuing others" if they are not already listed. If they are listed, circle them.

6. **Show the Cube.** Display the two different sayings on the cube – "GUILTY? THEN CHANGE" and VICTIM? THEN HANDLE IT. Explain that there are times that we may be guilty of hurtful behaviors – when that occurs we need to work on resisting or changing the behavior. On the other hand, there are times that we are the target or victim of someone else's hurtful actions – then we need to deal with it or handle it in an okay way.

7. Allow students to take turns rolling the cube. Instruct the person rolling the cube to be the group leader to lead a discussion of either a way to change when guilty of acting better than others and excluding people or to lead a discussion of ways to handle it when you are the target or victim of someone else excluding or being rude. The roll of the cube indicates which type of discussion. Continue rolling and discussing. Use the copy of the **QF (Quick Fix)** Summary Sheet to assist in the discussion – either referencing the sheet when in search of answers or handing a copy to each student to refer to and select an item to elaborate. Encourage the student to take and keep the QF sheet for future reference.

   The "What To Do" Cube will be used in other sessions to help explore both roles of bully (aggressive) behavior and target/victim and how to handle. Remember that girls typically end up on both sides of the problem at some point; therefore, it is important to explore both sides and give skills to help. Set aside the cube for use in future sessions.

8. **Closure:** Encourage each girl during the week to make a point to appreciate others' individuality, to compliment others, and to include different people in their activities.

Saved by the Bell

Kelly and I always talked together in the hallway before class. We'd been friends since kindergarten. Kelly suggested that today we join Allison's group in the hall – something about Allison had asked her for help with her math. I didn't know Allison that well but I agreed to go with Kelly. When we joined Allison's group, she said "hey" to Kelly and them looked at me, rolled her eyes and said, "Where did you get that lame outfit you're wearing?" I half-way smiled but felt like crawling in a hole. Everyone in her group was looking at me now and whispering. I felt like they were all talking about me. It hurt because these girls didn't even take the time to get to know me, they just made fun of my clothes. I was glad when the bell rang for class. Saved by the bell…

WHAT TO DO CUBE

Directions: To create the cube, cut along the dotted lines and fold along the solid lines. Fold in the shape of a cube and tape together. Allow the girls to take turns rolling the cube. Instruct the person rolling the cube to be the group leader to lead a discussion of either "change the behavior when guilty" or to discuss ways to "handle the behavior when you are a victim." The roll of the cube indicates which type of discussion. Continue taking turns, rolling the cube, and discussing. Use the copy of the QF (Quick Fix) Summary Sheet to assist in the discussion – either by referencing the sheet when in search of answers or for students to refer to the sheet to select an item to elaborate.

Guilty?
THEN CHANGE.

Victim?
THEN HANDLE IT.

Guilty?
THEN CHANGE.

Victim?
THEN HANDLE IT.

Victim?
THEN HANDLE IT.

Guilty?
THEN CHANGE.

QF (QUICK FIX) SUMMARY SHEET
for EXCLUSION
(leaving others out or being left out)

Guilty?
THEN CHANGE.

* Remind yourself that each person is different and unique. It is that difference that makes each person valuable, important, and special.

* Take the time to get to know the person - ask questions about what they like and really listen to what they say.

* Resist the temptation to exclude others or put others down to get your power. Empathize and care about others – think: "How would I feel if I was left out?"

* Invite the person to be a part of your group or activity.

* Other: _____

- -

Victim?
THEN HANDLE IT.

* Remind yourself that you don't need to be included by a certain group to be a worthwhile person.

* Remember Eleanor Roosevelt's words, "No one can make you feel inferior without your consent."

* Review your positive qualities and be proud of who you are.

* Get busy with other friends and other activities.

* Other: _____

GET THE "QF" on EXCLUSION
(leaving others out or being left out)

SESSION 3

GABBY GOSSIP vs. KIND COMPLIMENTS

Purpose:
To emphasize the importance of talking about others in a positive, kind way. Strategies for changing the hurtful behavior of gossip as well as dealing when you are the victim of gossip will be discussed.

Materials Needed:
Marker and poster of "Admirable Qualities" used in the previous session.

Copy of the Gossiping Pictures on pages 150-154. Fold the bottom half of the page away from the picture so that a person can hold the picture for others to see while reading the information on the back.

Copy for each student the QF (Quick Fix) Summary Sheet on page 155.

"What To Do Cube", page 147, from the previous session

Procedure:
1. **Review the previous lesson** and ask the students to share if they had a special opportunity to appreciate others and include others in activities.

2. **Ask what it means to gossip or spread rumors.** Explore the following: Why are we tempted to gossip? What can be a negative outcome of gossiping? How does it feel when you are the target of gossip?

3. **Share and discuss each of the Gossiping Picture Cards.** When each picture is folded it provides ease in holding the picture for others to see as you can view the written information on the back more easily to guide the discussion.

4. **Ask:** What is the opposite of gossip and rumors? Guide the answer to include – talking about people in a good way and sharing compliments. **Refer to the "Admirable Qualities" list** begun in Session 1 - add or circle "complimenting others" or "talking about others in a kind way".

5. Show the **"What To Do Cube"** with the sayings "GUILTY? THEN CHANGE" and VICTIM? THEN HANDLE IT. Allow students to take turns rolling the cube. Instruct the person rolling the cube to be the group leader to lead a discussion of either a way to change when guilty of gossiping or spreading rumors or to lead a discussion of ways to handle it when you are the target or victim of someone gossiping or spreading rumors. The roll of the cube indicates which type of discussion. Continue taking turns rolling and discussing. Use the copy of the QF (Quick Fix) Summary Sheet to assist in the discussion – either referencing the sheet when in search of answers or handing a copy to each student to refer to and select an item to elaborate. Encourage the student to take and keep the QF sheet for future reference.

(told here)

DISCUSSION INFORMATION:

1. Ask the following questions to guide the discussion:
   - What do you think is happening in the picture?
   - How do you think the girls involved in the gossiping feel?
   - Do you think anyone in the picture might be uncomfortable? If so, why?
   - If Hannah knew they were talking about her, how do you think she would feel?

2. Explain that turn around statements can be used to counteract with something good about the girl that is being gossiped about rather than agreeing with the gossip. Ask for an example of a turn around statement that could be used in this situation.

3. Explain that changing the subject is another strategy that can be used to avoid participating in gossiping. Rather than asking questions or saying something back about the gossip you can change the subject by complimenting the person's shoes and asking where she got them or by sharing something about a recent movie at the theaters. Ask the group to give examples of how they might change the subject.

DISCUSSION INFORMATION:

1. Share with the girls that prior to this scene earlier in the day, Jordan, the girl showing the text message, had sent a text message to Caroline asking her what she thought of Kelly. Jordan was jealous of Caroline and Kelly's friendship so she saved the message to show Caroline in hopes that it would cause a problem between the two.

2. Ask:

   ■ What is your reaction to the situation?
   ■ Do you feel it was right of Jordan to share the text message? Why or why not?
   ■ Have you ever been tempted to say something not so nice about someone because you thought that is what they wanted to hear?

Kelly, look
what Caroline
said about you

DISCUSSION INFORMATION:

1. Ask:
   ■ What do you see happening in the picture? Where can the message be sent when you press the "forward" button in your email?
   ■ Do you always have control over where your email may end up when you send a message to someone?
   ■ Do you think someone might choose to forward the message on to Jillian? What problems could it cause?

2. Explain that before you consider passing on a rumor or gossip it must first pass through these three questions:
   ■ Is it true? (If it isn't don't say it. If it is move ahead to the next two questions.)
   ■ Is it necessary to say?
   ■ Is it kind? (If it is not necessary to say it, don't say it. If it is necessary to say then find a kind way to say it.)

..... (fold here) ....

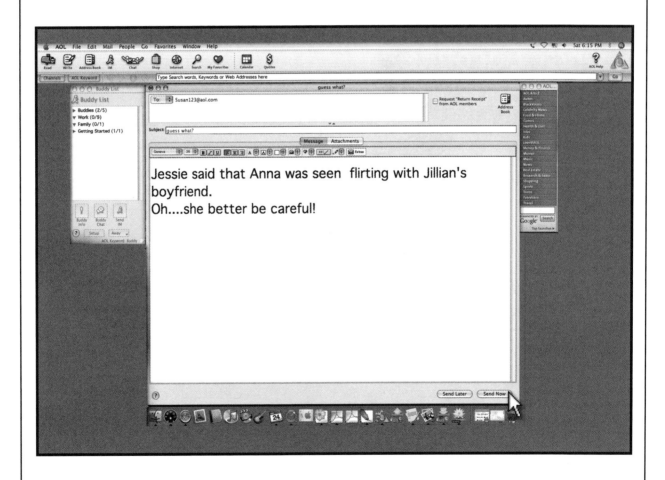

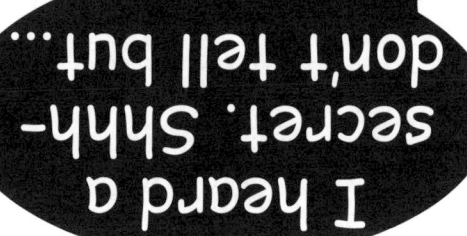

I heard a secret. Shhh- don't tell but....

(fold here)

DISCUSSION INFORMATION:

1. Ask:
   - What do you see happening in the picture?
   - Has one of your secrets ever been shared by someone else?
   - Have you ever passed on a secret you were asked not to tell? Why?

2. ANSWER **TRUE** or **FALSE** for the following statements:
   a. It's okay to tell a secret someone told you if you make the person promise not to tell anyone.
   b. It's okay to tell a secret someone told you if the secret is likely to get out anyway.
   c. It's okay to tell a secret someone told you if you don't mention anyone's name but talk in general terms instead.
   d. It's okay to tell a secret someone told you if someone is in danger or hurting themselves.

   Discuss how a.-c. are false and d. is true.

(fold here)

DISCUSSION INFORMATION:

1. Ask:
- What's happening in these two pictures?
- Tonya is the girl who is in both pictures. What do you think motivates her to ask and then pass on the information? (Bring out in the discussion the possibility that Tonya may be seeking information to have power and improve her status with the group.
- Can Tonya be trusted with personal information?
- How do you think Kelsey will feel when she finds out Tonya is passing on information?

Oh Kelsey, what do you think about....?

Do you know what Kelsey just said?

QF (QUICK FIX) SUMMARY SHEET
for RUMORS AND GOSSIPS

Guilty?
THEN CHANGE.

* Assume that what you say behind someone's back will get back to the person.

* Try changing the subject when someone shares a rumor or tries to gossip with you.

* When you are tempted to gossip – say something nice about the person instead.

* Watch what you put in writing…

* Stop and think what you should say before you say it.

* If you have passed on an untrue rumor, apologize and then go to those you gossiped to and set the story straight.

* Resist temptation to tell your friend's secret – remain a person that can be trusted.

* Other: _____

Victim?
THEN HANDLE IT.

* Let your real friends know it's not true.

* Laugh it off.

* Label it as a ridiculous rumor.

* Don't take it personally, realize it may have resulted from someone's need for power or control.

* Resist the urge for revenge – you're better than that!

* Other: _____

GET THE "QF" on RUMORS and GOSSIP!

SESSION 4

HURTFUL TEASING vs. CARING COMMUNICATION

Purpose:

To emphasize the importance of communicating in a caring way. Strategies for changing the hurtful behavior of teasing as well as dealing when you are the victim of teasing will be discussed.

Materials Needed:

Copy and cut apart the "Teasing Role Plays".

Marker and poster of "Admirable Qualities" used in previous session

Copy for each student the QF (Quick Fix) Summary Sheet on page 159.

"What To Do" Cube, page 147

Procedure:

1. Allow each group member to **share** their answer to the following question: What is one thing great about being a girl?

2. **Ask:** Are there different types of teasing? Differentiate between hurtful teasing and okay, fun teasing. Explain that the difference lies with the intent, if there is intent to hurt or harm then it is hurtful teasing. Point out that hurtful teasing includes laughter directed "at" the target, not "with" the target and usually continues even though the person objects.

3. **Distribute the Teasing Role Play strips** and take turns role playing and discussing. Include both sides in the discussion by asking if they have been guilty of hurtful teasing and if they have been the target of hurtful teasing. Discuss how it felt and what thoughts went through your mind about the situation. Explore reasons why people may tease in a hurtful way.

4. **Discussion Situations:** Read the following teasing situations and discuss the feelings and thoughts about the situation. Have the group replace the teasing remark with a caring statement.

   ❋ You had been in a car accident several years ago and have had surgery on your crushed ankle twice. The injury has left you walking with a limp. Frequently, others give you a hard time about how you walk laughing at you and saying, "Here comes our beauty queen gliding down the runway with her smooth walk!"

✳ Your parents are getting divorced and you are devastated – you always thought they would be together forever. It's parents day at school and both parents are invited to attend the class presentation but because your parents can't get along and be in the same room together right now neither parent attends. A classmate makes the comment, "What, no one is here for you…no one loves you…?"

✳ You have a speech problem and everyone makes fun of you. Your classmates have said things like…, "You talk like a baby." Or "What, are you tongue tied!?"

4. **Ask:** What is the opposite of hurtful teasing? Guide the answer to include communicating or talking in a caring way. **Refer to the "Admirable Qualities"** list begun in Session 1 - add or circle "talking in a caring way".

5. Show the **"What To Do Cube"** with the sayings "GUILTY? THEN CHANGE" and VICTIM? THEN HANDLE IT. Allow students to take turns rolling the cube. Instruct the person rolling the cube to be the group leader to lead a discussion of either a way to change when guilty of hurtful teasing or to lead a discussion of ways to handle it when you are the target or victim of being teased in a hurtful way. The roll of the cube indicates which type of discussion. Continue taking turns rolling and discussing. Use the copy of the **QF (Quick Fix) Summary Sheet** to assist in the discussion – either referencing the sheet when in search of answers or handing a copy to each student to refer to and select an item to elaborate. Encourage the student to take and keep the QF sheet for future reference.

TEASING ROLE PLAYS

Directions:

Copy and cut apart each role-play situation. Role-play each and discuss.

Role Play 1

Person 1: That outfit you're wearing looks like it came from the second hand store.

Person 2: What? (*display a look of hurt and confusion*)

Person 1: Just kidding!

Role Play 2

Person 1: Mia said that you are the worst friend ever.

Person 2: Why did she say that? (*distressed look*)

Person 1: Sike!

Role Play 3

Person 1: You are so out of style and lame, you don't fit with our group.

Person 2: Who cares about your group?

Person 1: Obviously you, you're still here.

Role Play 4

Person 1: Loser, loser – you're a real zero! Go join the loser's club.

Person 2: (*silent*)

QF (QUICK FIX) SUMMARY SHEET
for HURTFUL TEASING

Guilty?
**THEN
CHANGE.**

* Think before you speak. Think how you may feel if someone said the hurtful statement to you.

* When tempted, get involved in a different activity.

* Stop yourself before you say it and turn it around to a compliment instead.

* If a hurtful statement is said, apologize.

* Other: _____

Victim?
**THEN
HANDLE IT.**

* Ask the person to stop.

* Walk away.

* Ignore, look bored.

* Resist the temptation to say something cruel back – don't lower to their level.

* Possible statements:
"Yea, right – funny." *(with serious face)*
"That's your opinion not mine."
"And I would care because…?"

* Remember, don't believe what they are saying… just because they say it doesn't make it true.

* If the teasing is constant, mark on a calendar when it happens and let an adult know.

* Other: _____

GET THE "QF" on HURTFUL TEASING!

SESSION 5

BOSSING, CONTROLLING, INTIMIDATING vs. RESPECT AND EMPATHY

Purpose:

To emphasize the importance of developing respect and empathy toward others. Strategies for changing the hurtful behavior of bossing, controlling, and intimidating as well as dealing when you are the victim will be discussed.

Materials Needed:

Hand held mirror

Construction paper/cardstock "Reputation Mirror" copied and cut out for each girl.

Marker and poster of "Admirable Qualities" used in previous sessions.

Copy for each student the QF (Quick Fix) Summary Sheet on page 163.

"What To Do" Cube, page 147

Procedure:

1. Ask each girl to **share** the following: *One thing that is hard about being a girl.*

2. **Tell a Story Activity:** Explain to the group that you will give the topic of a story to create. Begin with the line, "Once upon a time a…" then turn to a group member for her to add a line. Each girl can then add an additional sentence to the story. Summarize the story and discuss.

    STORY STARTERS:
    * "Once upon a time my friend was very bossy. She…"
    * "Once upon a time my friend was very controlling, always telling everyone what to do. She…"
    * "Once upon a time my friend was very intimidating. It scared me when she…"
    * "Once upon a time my friend manipulated me. She…"

3. Explain that empathy is understanding what others are experiencing – how they are thinking and feeling about a situation. **Read the situations below.** Discuss how you would feel if…
    * You are a new student at school and don't know anyone. In the cafeteria you ask to sit with a group of girls and they say, "Get lost – go back where you came from." They all laugh.
    * You have been assigned to partner with one of the most popular girls to complete a science project. At school you have set three different meeting times to research for the project but she never shows. Two days before it is due she calls you and says, "I am so sorry I haven't met with you about the project. You are so smart and always do a good job. I trust you to do a good job with the project and I'll just add my name. Thanks."

✳ You were just talking to Steve answering his questions about the math class that he missed, when Allison pulled you away and said, "If you come around my boyfriend again, you'll regret it!"

✳ Elizabeth and you are friends but every time you try to talk to or hang out with someone else she always gets mad.

4. **Present the word, REPUTATION.** Ask the girls to define. Conclude with a definition similar to: How others see us by how we act over and over again. Point out that reputations can be positive or negative – a person may have the reputation as being kind, caring, helpful, trustworthy, organized, responsible, etc. or a person may have a negative reputation as being mean, cruel, bossy, manipulative, a snob, etc.

5. **Hold a mirror** up and recall the mirror used in the story of Snow White. Explain that this mirror is a little different in that when you look into it you can ask the question, **"Mirror, mirror in my hand what is my reputation – where do I stand?"** Ask the girls to quietly review their own behavior – you may encourage them to share offering support for their honesty and encouraging change. **Hand each girl a prepared paper mirror.** Ask each girl to write their name on the handle and then write on the mirror the type of reputation they would like to have. Allow the girls to share. Discuss with the girls how she would need to act over and over again to have that reputation.

6. **Ask:** *What is the opposite of bossing, controlling, and intimidating?* Guide the answer to include showing care and empathy. Refer to the "Admirable Qualities" list begun in Session 1 - add or circle "care and empathy".

7. Show the **"What To Do Cube"** with the sayings "GUILTY? THEN CHANGE" and VICTIM? THEN HANDLE IT. Allow students to take turns rolling the cube. Instruct the person rolling the cube to be the group leader to lead a discussion of either a way to change when guilty of bossing, controlling, or intimidating or to lead a discussion of ways to handle it when you are the target or victim of being bossed, controlled or intimidated. The roll of the cube indicates which type of discussion. Continue taking turns rolling and discussing. Use the copy of the QF **(Quick Fix) Summary Sheet** to assist in the discussion – either referencing the sheet when in search of answers or handing a copy to each student to refer to and select an item to elaborate. Encourage the student to take and keep the QF sheet for future reference.

8. Review the **Kind Deeds Assignment Sheet.** Assign or allow the girls to choose one kind deed to follow through and complete in the upcoming week. Tell them they need to be prepared at the next meeting to share the results – what happened, how the person may have felt or what they may have thought about the good deed, and about how you felt or thought after you completed the kind deed. (Since you may not be doing the sessions in order, I will not include a reminder to process this activity in the next session. However, you may want to make a note for yourself to process this assignment at the beginning of the next meeting.)

REPUTATION MIRROR

$\mathcal{D}$irections:
Copy and cut out the mirror. Describe a positive reputation you would like to have – write this information on the mirror part. You may include information such as: caring, helpful, friendly, trustworthy, honest, respectful, kind, responsible, etc. Next describe how you would have to act in order to have that reputation.

Mirror, mirror in my hand,   What is my reputation?

Where do I stand?

QF (QUICK FIX) SUMMARY SHEET
for HURTFUL TEASING

Guilty?
THEN CHANGE.

❋ Remind yourself of the good reputation you are striving for and how you need to act each day to achieve that good reputation.

❋ Put yourself in the other person's place - would you want to be treated in that way?

❋ Other: _____

- -

Victim?
THEN HANDLE IT.

❋ Use assertive skills and tell her to stop.

❋ Value yourself – remind yourself that you are not the problem.

❋ You may choose to say something like: "I'm sorry you're having a bad day."

❋ Other: _____

GET THE "QF" on BOSSING, CONTROLLING, and INTIMIDATING!

KIND DEEDS
ASSIGNMENT SHEET

Directions:
Put a check mark beside the kind deed that you will complete in the upcoming week.

☐ Send a compliment note to a classmate telling something they do well.

☐ Find a student who seems to be alone at recess and offer to be his/her friend. Continue to talk with that person and show your friendliness.

☐ Sit with someone different in the lunchroom or on the bus.

☐ Write and send a thank you note to your parent.

☐ Do an extra chore around the house to help out your parents.

☐ Tell a cafeteria worker "thank you" for their hard work!

☐ Send a "thinking of you" note/card to your grandparents, aunt, uncle, or another adult friend.

☐ Do something extra nice for a brother or sister.

SESSION 6 · FRIENDSHIP BETRAYAL vs. HONESTY AND LOYALTY

Purpose:
To emphasize the importance of being honest and loyal to a friend. Strategies for changing the hurtful behavior of betraying a friend as well as dealing when you are the victim will be discussed.

Materials Needed:
Copy of the book, My Secret Bully by T. Ludwig

Toothpaste and a sheet of paper or paper plate

Marker and poster of "Admirable Qualities" used in previous lessons (chart originated in Session 1)

Copy for each student the QF (Quick Fix) Summary Sheet on page 167.

"What To Do Cube", page 147

Procedure:
1. Present the following **situations for discussion:**
   * On again, off again friends – one minute we are best friends, the next she doesn't seem to want to speak to me.
   * Sometimes I feel like my friend is just "using" me.
   * It's really weird, she seems to be my friend in the neighborhood but she doesn't seem to want to be my friend at school.

   Share the following advice from Lindsay, age 14: "When a good friend turns against you it hurts – there is pain, anger, humiliation, and confusion. IT HURTS when someone who I thought was my friend and who I trusted with my feelings, thoughts, and secrets turned out to use it against me and betray our friendship. It's hard not to take it personal, but there is a bigger picture out there that may have nothing to do with me. It is amazing what some girls will do for fear of not fitting in and belonging to a popular group – I think it's more important to value who you are and how you treat people than it is to resort to hurtful behavior to gain status. Remember, if this ever happens to you, don't seek revenge – it's not worth it - and don't blame yourself."

2. **Share the book,** My Secret Bully by T. Ludwig. Discuss the story.

3. **Ask:** *Is there a difference between not being friends because "friendships change and we grow in different directions" and not being friends because of "betrayal, being used, and power seeking with other groups"? If so, how?*

4. Share the following **toothpaste analogy** (borrowed analogy - source unknown): Ask a girl to squirt some toothpaste out on a piece of paper or paper plate. Ask if it was easy to do. Next, hand her the tube of toothpaste back and ask her to put every bit of the toothpaste back in the tube just the way it was. This is an impossible task. Summarize how it was easy to get it out but impossible to get it all back. Relate this to friends in how it may be easy to say all kinds of things – even things that are hurtful but we need to be careful because once they are said you can't take it back. Point out that not even an apology can remove the words totally.

5. **Refer to the "Admirable Qualities" Chart and ask:** What is the positive admirable trait that is the opposite of friendship betrayal? Guide the answer to include being honest and loyal to a friend. Refer to the "Admirable Qualities" list begun in Session 1 - add or circle "honest and loyal".

6. Show the **"What To Do" Cube** with the sayings "GUILTY? THEN CHANGE" and VICTIM? THEN HANDLE IT. Allow students to take turns rolling the cube. Instruct the person rolling the cube to be the group leader to lead a discussion of either a way to change when guilty of betraying or using a friend or to lead a discussion of ways to handle it when you are the target or victim of being betrayed or used. The roll of the cube indicates which type of discussion. Continue taking turns rolling and discussing. Use the copy of the QF (Quick Fix) Summary Sheet to assist in the discussion – either referencing the sheet when in search of answers or handing a copy to each student to refer to and select an item to elaborate. Encourage the student to take and keep the QF sheet for future reference.

QF (QUICK FIX) SUMMARY SHEET
for FRIENDSHIP BETRAYAL

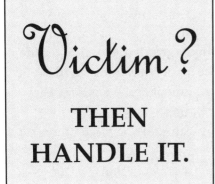

Guilty?
THEN CHANGE.

* Fight the urge to share someone's private or personal information just to fit in or be popular.

* Resist the urge to seek revenge on a friend. Get the facts - she may not have done what you think she did. If she did do the wrong, then remember that two wrongs don't make a right.

* Remember the toothpaste analogy.

* Other: _____

Victim?
THEN HANDLE IT.

* Hold your head high and appreciate your good values.

* Remember that the hurt will heal.

* Assertively confront the friend.

* Forgive, forget, and move on. Holding resentment and anger is not worth it.

* Rebuild your ability to trust – not everyone will mistreat the trust.

* Other: _____

GET THE "QF" on FRIENDSHIP BETRAYAL!

SESSION 7 — CAUGHT IN THE MIDDLE

Purpose:

To review helpful strategies when you are "caught in the middle" between friends.

Materials Needed:

Write each of the sayings in #2 on poster strips.

Copy and cut apart the "Caught In the Middle" Situations on page 169.

Pencils/pens and a copy of the "Think, Say, or Do" Sheet for each student

Procedure:

1. **Ask:** What does it mean to be caught in the middle with friends? Encourage the girls to share thoughts, feelings, and personal experiences.

2. Display the following **poster strip sayings and ask what they think each means:**
   * "It takes courage not to go along with the friend with the power."
   * "You have to like yourself when you look in the mirror."
   * "Sometimes you have to make unpopular choices."
   * "To be a real friend means _____."

3. Have each of the girls take turns drawing a paper slip and **leading a group discussion on the "Caught in the Middle"** Situations. (Allowing the girls to take the leadership role provides you an opportunity to see her skills and interactions with others. Compliment and encourage each student as they take on the role of the leader and participant for both are needed roles in friendships. Don't forget to encourage eye contact, head nods, and summarizing what others say.)

4. Ask the girls to **complete the "Think, Say, or Do" Worksheet** to list ways to think, or things to say, or do in order to handle it when you are caught in the middle. Allow time for students to share their answers.

TEASING ROLE PLAYS

Directions:
Copy and cut apart the following situations. Allow each girl to select a situation and lead a group discussion on how to handle.

One of your good friends, Emily, starting making fun of Cynthia, one of your classmates in math class. You could see that Cynthia was really hurt by what Emily was saying and it wasn't right of Emily to be so mean… but Emily is a good friend of yours. What would you do?

You are trying so hard to be a part and fit in with this one group at school. You had finally gotten to the place that they included you when they gathered in the hall to talk. One morning Teri, a neighborhood friend, saw you and stopped to speak to you. At that moment, Elaina turned to Teri and said, "Who do you think you are? No one invited you to join our group?" Teri was horrified, she looked at me and… What would you do?

My two best friends, Angie and Sutton, were mad at each other and I was caught in the middle. Angie would stop me at lunch and talk bad about Sutton. Sutton would talk to me in the halls and try to turn me against Angie. What would you do if you were me?

I wanted to be accepted as a friend by Marilyn, she had a sharp edge to her but everyone thought she was so cool. I was at the lockers with Marilyn when Jackie an old friend walked by. Marilyn turned around and didn't hesitate to cut her down about her wimpy clothes. Marilyn turned to me and said, "Rather than Jackie looking like "the bomb" in her clothes it looks like a bomb went off on her clothes." She laughed and turned to me and expected me to join in laughing. I worked so hard to get accepted by Marilyn… I'm tempted to join in… What would you do?

THINK, SAY, or DO
W O R K S H E E T

When I am caught in the middle between friends I can…

WHAT TO THINK:

_____

_____

_____

_____

WHAT TO SAY:

_____

_____

_____

_____

WHAT TO DO:

_____

_____

_____

_____

SESSION 8

THE TRUE ME

Purpose:
To build our confidence by affirming our abilities, capabilities, and values.

Materials Needed:
Copy of the Positive Self-Talk Affirmation Statements for each girl

10 index cards, a pen/pencil, and a small plastic bag for each girl

List of "Admirable Qualities" used in previous sessions

Poster board strip of the statement "Seek popularity not based on power but popularity based on admirable qualities." used in Session 2

Procedure:
1. **Ask each girl to share:** What is one thing that is special or unique about you - something that you are good at and have to offer others?

2. **Explain that our goal is to have confidence** in ourselves. Share that confidence provides us with power about who we are so we don't resort to bully behavior to gain power. And, confidence allows up to develop healthy ways to handle hurtful behavior when we are a target/victim.

3. Share that one way to build confidence is to affirm our abilities, capabilities, and value through **Positive Self-Talk Affirmation Statements**. Hand each student a list of the Positive Self-Talk Affirmation samples, ten index cards, pen/pencil, and a plastic bag to hold the cards. Instruct the girls to review the possible self-talk positive affirmation statements on the sheet and select those that may be true and helpful for her. Ask the girls to write 10 of the affirmation statements – one on each index card. They are welcome to use the statements from the sheet or create their own. Next, allow the girls to read aloud their statements. Assign for each girl to take her bag of affirmation cards with her, and to select a card each day to read aloud in the morning, perhaps put on the bathroom mirror or carry during the day and read several more times. Add a new card each day.

4. **Revisit the "Admirable Qualities" list** that was completed in prior sessions. Also **review the statement,** "Seek popularity not based on power but on admirable qualities." Ask each girl to assess where she is in this process.

Positive Self-Talk Affirmations

I am an honest person.

I can be trusted.

I can show respect for myself and others.

I am a caring person.

I am kind to others.

I know how to be a good listener.

I know how to be a good friend.

I am smart.

I can make responsible choices.

I have the courage to face the problems in my day.

I can handle this.

I will share my smile with others today.

I can take the time to say nice things to others.

I am a valuable person.

I believe in myself.

I am a good person.

I will choose to be happy today.

I will not give in to peer pressure.

I accept people for who they are, not what they look like.

I like who I am.

SESSION 9

FRIENDSHIP CONFLICTS: PROBLEM SOLVERS TO THE RESCUE

Purpose:

To review the difference between a conflict problem and a bully problem, to reinforce positive conflict management strategies, and to learn how to make and accept an apology.

Materials Needed:

Pencil/pen and a copy of the Conflict-Solvers Quiz, Friendly Conflict Situations, and Apology Sheet for each student

Chart paper or poster board and marker

Procedure:

1. **Share the following:** Conflicts are disagreements or problems that come up with others. We can have conflicts with our friends without it being a bullying problem. Remember, with bullying behavior there is intent to hurt or harm which is not true of all conflicts. Conflicts can arise when each person has different needs or wants that are in opposition with each other. Conflicts are a normal part of our friendships and our life, bullying is not. When these conflicts arise we can find appropriate strategies to resolve.

2. **Ask:** *What are some typical friendship conflicts or problems?* You may begin the sharing by giving examples of: disagreement about a movie to watch, your friend forgets about plans made, or something said by accident that hurt someone's feelings.

3. Explain that we each have different styles we use to deal with conflicts. **Hand to each student the "Conflict-Solvers Quiz."** Direct the students to answer each question by circling her typical style in handling conflicts. Discuss the pros and cons of each approach.

4. **Ask:** *What are some helpful strategies you use to handle friendship conflicts?* Make a list on newsprint or poster board. The list may include such strategies as: send an "I" message – talk it out, ignore, get the facts, apologize, humor, compromise, take turns, share, or get help.

5. **Hand out the "Friendly Conflict Situations".** Allow the students to work in pairs. Assign a situation for each pair to review and determine helpful conflict management strategies. Students are encouraged to refer to the list of helpful strategies created earlier. You may choose to verbally add other friendship conflicts that were shared earlier. Allow time for students to read their conflict situations to the group and share their strategies.

6. Hand to each student a copy of the **"Apology Sheet"**. Explain that we do make mistakes sometimes and say or do things that we shouldn't. Share that being able to apologize and communicate to others that you are sorry as well as knowing how to accept an apology is important. Review the information on the apology sheet together. Encourage the students to take the sheet with them as a review/reminder of the lesson.

CONFLICT-SOLVERS
QUIZ

Directions:
Circle the part of the sentence that is your correct answer.

When you have a conflict with a friend do you typically…

1.
Text message or email her the concern
OR
talk face to face?

2.
Ignore the problem
OR
talk it out?

3.
Ask others and involve them
OR
keep it just between those directly involved?

4.
Jump to conclusions
OR
ask questions to get the facts?

5.
Blame others totally
OR
admit your part and apologize?

FRIENDSHIP CONFLICT SITUATIONS

Directions:

Review the conflict situations and decide helpful conflict management strategies to use.
Write these in the spaces provided.

1. A friend thinks she is being funny, but her comments about your new shoes really bothers you.

   Conflict Management Strategies to use:

   _____

   _____

2. You have a disagreement about what movie to watch.

   Conflict Management Strategies to use:

   _____

   _____

3. When you make plans with your friend to meet, she is always late. This bothers you.

   Conflict Management Strategies to use:

   _____

   _____

4. Your friend is acting like she is mad at you but you have no idea what you may have done.

   Conflict Management Strategies to use:

   _____

   _____

5. Your friend borrowed your new CD but dropped and scratched it.

   Conflict Management Strategies to use:

   _____

   _____

APOLOGY

TO MAKE AN APOLOGY, CONSIDER THE FOLLOWING:

* Be specific about what you did wrong

* No blaming or excuses

* Use words and show with your body language that you are sorry

* Let her know what you should have done and what you will do differently next time

* Let her know that you value your friendship

TO ACCEPT AN APOLOGY, CONSIDER THE FOLLOWING:

* Listen, hear her out

* Don't go over or get into the argument again

* Accept the words of apology and time will show if it was sincere

* Review if you need to apologize for your part in the problem

SESSION 10	FABULOUS FRIENDSHIPS

Purpose:

To reinforce the importance of good friends and friendships. This session also includes the post assessment used to determine the degree to which the student is implementing the skills learned in the group.

Materials Needed:

Chart paper or poster board and marker

Pencil/pen and a copy of the Student Post Assessment for each girl

Copies of the Parent/Teacher Post Assessment if utilizing

Procedure:

1. Make a list of **good things about friends and friendships.**

2. **Summarize the group experience** allowing students to share. Ask them to share one thing that they will do differently because of this group.

3. Hand out the **Student Post Assessment** for students to complete. If you involved the teacher and parents with the pre-assessment, then send them the Parent Post Assessment to complete. Compile the information to determine the degree to which the student is implementing the skills learned and to plan follow-up if needed.

4. End the group session with a **"hot-seat" activity**. Take turns pretending for a student to be in the selected "hot seat" and ask each other girl to give one compliment or share something the student does well. Rotate until everyone has had a turn. Thank the girls for participating.

STUDENT POST ASSESSMENT
for SURVIVING AND THRIVING IN THE GIRL WORLD

Student Name: _____ Date: _____

Directions: Complete the following post assessment reflecting your present skills.
Mark your answers honestly.

		4 *strongly agree*	**3** *agree*	**2** *disagree*	**1** *strongly disagree*
1.	I understand what is meant by being in the "Girl World".	❏	❏	❏	❏
2a.	I appreciate and include others rather than leaving others out or excluding them.	❏	❏	❏	❏
2b.	I know how to handle it when others leave me out.	❏	❏	❏	❏
3a.	I only say nice things about others and I resist the temptation to spread rumors and gossip.	❏	❏	❏	❏
3b.	I know how to handle it when others spread rumors and gossip about me.	❏	❏	❏	❏
4a.	I enjoy talking in a caring way with others rather than teasing and making fun of people.	❏	❏	❏	❏
4b.	I know how to handle it when people tease and make fun of me.	❏	❏	❏	❏
5a.	I show respect and empathy for others and do not boss or take advantage of people.	❏	❏	❏	❏
5b.	I know how to handle it when others boss or try to take advantage of me.	❏	❏	❏	❏
6a.	I am loyal and honest with others and do not betray or talk bad about people behind their back.	❏	❏	❏	❏
6b.	I know how to handle it if others betray me or talk bad about me behind my back.	❏	❏	❏	❏
7.	I know how to handle it if I am "caught in the middle" between friends.	❏	❏	❏	❏
8.	I like myself, I am a good person, and I value who I am.	❏	❏	❏	❏
9.	I know how to handle conflicts or disagreements, in helpful ways.	❏	❏	❏	❏
10.	I know how to be a good friend to others.	❏	❏	❏	❏

11. In this group experience I learned: _____

_____

12. The most helpful part of the group was: _____

_____

13. In order to be more helpful, I would recommend that you change or add to the small group by:

_____

PARENT / TEACHER LETTER

Dear Parent/Teacher,

We are concluding our small group on Surviving and Thriving in the Girl World. We have focused on the skills of:

I have enjoyed working with _____ and will continue to offer support during the year. To help assess the degree to which your child is implementing the skills learned, please complete the post assessment listed below and return. Your answers need to reflect the student's present behavior. Thank you.

Sincerely,

Your School Counselor

PARENT/TEACHER PRE ASSESSMENT *for* SURVIVING AND THRIVING IN THE GIRL WORLD GROUP

Student Name: _____ Date: _____

		4 *strongly agree*	**3** *agree*	**2** *disagree*	**1** *strongly disagree*
1.	She understands what is meant by being in the "Girl World".	❑	❑	❑	❑
2a.	She appreciates and includes others rather than leaving others out or excluding them.	❑	❑	❑	❑
2b.	She knows how to handle it when others leave her out.	❑	❑	❑	❑
3a.	She only says nice things about others and she resists the temptation to spread rumors and gossip.	❑	❑	❑	❑
3b.	She knows how to handle it when others spread rumors and gossip about her.	❑	❑	❑	❑
4a.	She enjoys talking in a caring way with others rather than teasing and making fun of people.	❑	❑	❑	❑
4b.	She knows how to handle it when others tease and make fun of her.	❑	❑	❑	❑
5a.	She shows respect and empathy for others and does not boss or take advantage of people.	❑	❑	❑	❑
5b.	She knows how to handle it when others boss or tries to take advantage of her.	❑	❑	❑	❑
6a.	She is loyal and honest with others and does not betray or talk bad about people behind their back.	❑	❑	❑	❑
6b.	She knows how to handle it when others betray her.	❑	❑	❑	❑
7.	She knows how to handle it if she is "caught in the middle" between friends.	❑	❑	❑	❑
8.	She likes herself, she is a good person, and she values who she is.	❑	❑	❑	❑
9.	She knows how to handle conflicts or disagreements in helpful ways.	❑	❑	❑	❑
10.	She knows how to be a good friend to others.	❑	❑	❑	❑

Comments: _____

CHAPTER 5

Individual Counseling Activities on Girl Bullying

Bullying involves the three roles: the role of bully behavior, the target/victim, and the bystander. Girls can bully through overt, open means of hurting each other such as pushing, threatening, "in your face" behavior or they can bully through more covert methods of exclusion, rumors, gossips, behind the back action, controlling, and manipulating. In counseling, we strive to assist the girl in whatever role they may be "playing" at the time and to help them find a healthy approach to valuing themselves and others.

The counseling activities in this section address various issues associated with girl bullying such as: valuing who we are, strengthening our friendship skills, supporting healthy strategies to deal with being a target/victim of bullying behavior, prompting to review our own behavior and make changes, and building empathy. Our goal of individual counseling is to encourage each girl to seek value and power in healthy, appropriate ways showing respect for herself and others. Review the purpose of the activities to determine if the activity matches the specific need of the individual student.

The following information provides the activities and approaches to address the problem, it is your insight and counseling skills that are needed. As the counselor, you can use your skills to "hear the words beneath the words". Utilize good counseling skills of reflective listening, head nods, using open questions, using encouraging statements, summarizing, clarifying, and gentle confrontations. Work to understand the student from the student's perspective – from her world. You can observe her affect to help guide her in understanding and movement towards resolution and positive mental health.

As always when working with students in individual counseling, remember our ethical standards including confidentiality and referring out when needed.

LIKING YOURSELF –
Be a Friend to Yourself and Others

Purpose:

To like who we are and realize that we first have to be our own best friend before we can be friends with others.

Materials Needed:

Paper and pencil/pen

Procedures:

Ask the student: ***What qualities in a friend do you value?*** Write these qualities on paper. Include such qualities as: caring, helpful, honest, trustworthy, loyal, a good listener, encouraging, and enjoys doing things together.

Ask the student what she thinks the following statement means: "Be your own best friend." Clarify that we must first like ourselves and be a good friend to ourselves in order to be a good friend to others. Point out that we must be honest with ourselves, care about ourselves, encourage ourselves, and enjoy being with ourselves. Ask the student to share some activities she enjoys doing by herself.

Engage in a discussion with the following questions:
- *Are friends someone you like?*
- *Do you like yourself?*
- *What about yourself do you like?*
- *What do you have to offer yourself and others?*

Return to the original list of friendship qualities. Circle the qualities that the student feels she already possesses – add any additional qualities. Ask the student to give examples of why she feels she possesses the friendship quality and encourage her to appreciate and compliment her good qualities.

Allow her to take the list as a visual reminder of her friendship qualities

FRIENDLY CONNECTIONS

Purpose:
To become more aware of our body language and words and the role it plays in connecting with friends.

Materials Needed:
Mirror

Situation cards copied and cut apart

Procedures:
Ask the student if she has ever been in a situation where she did not know anyone – a new student in class, at a birthday party, a large family reunion. Discuss the feelings involved and how she may have handled the situation. Explain that sometimes it is hard to know what to say or do with others.

Discuss the saying "a picture is worth a thousand words". Reference the saying to our body language (the picture of our face) and the message that it sends. Introduce different feeling words asking the student to communicate the feeling with her facial/body expressions. Use the mirror to review the facial expression to see if the student agrees that it communicated what she intended.

Also, introduce the concept of "self-talk". Explain that self-talk is what we think or say to ourselves about a situation. Our self-talk will affect our feelings and how we handle ourselves. Emphasize the importance of positive self-talk to help us deal with new or difficult situations.

Refer to the situation cards. Explain that each card lists a situation with negative self-talk and role play and then a positive self talk and re-play. Review each card and role play/replay the situation. Discuss the difference between the two scenes pointing out the positive body language that is more conducive to connecting with others and opening statements that can be used.

Successfully connecting with others is a good feeling however review with the student that at times, even with our best efforts, we do not always successfully connect. Discuss ways to handle and deal with the situation when it is not successful.

Depending on the needs of the student, create additional situation cards that could include: coming into a room with arms folded and a pout on the face, or coming in the room but pulling a seat away from the group to sit by yourself, or coming into a room with a bad attitude/angry look on the face.

Situation:

It's the first day of middle school and it's lunch time. There are three different lunch times and you don't know which or if any of your friends will have the same lunch. You enter the table area with your lunch and…

NEGATIVE SELF-TALK: "Oh no…this will be a disaster if I don't know anyone. People will think I'm a loser and laugh at me. I know, I'll get a cocky look on my face and just pretend to laugh at them first."

ROLE PLAY: Come into the room with a hand up to the mouth and pretend to laugh at others. Add a few eye rolls.

. . . .

POSITIVE SELF-TALK: "I'll just put a smile on my face and work on making new friends to eat lunch with. After all it is the first day, I bet I'm not the only one nervous about this."

RE-PLAY: Come into the room with a pleasant look on your face with good eye contact. Sit down by some others you may want to get to know and say, "Hi, I'm _____."

Situation:

It's the first day of changing classes where everyone seems to have a different class. After figuring out your schedule and finding your room number you…

NEGATIVE SELF-TALK: "I am so nervous and embarrassed about going into class. What if I don't know anyone? Everyone is going to stare at me."

ROLE PLAY: Hesitate coming in the room with your head down and no eye contact. Grab the first seat you come to, open your book, and stare into it.

. . . .

POSITIVE SELF-TALK: "I am a little nervous about a new class, but I will smile and speak to people. I will work on getting to know others and will allow others to get to know the good part of me."

RE-PLAY: Come in the room with your head up, pleasant look on your face, and good eye contact with others. Sit down next to someone and ask, "Hey, how are you?"

FRIENDSHIP RIPPLE*

Purpose:

To understand how our attitude whether positive or negative can affect ourselves and others.

Materials Needed:

Copy of the "Ripple Effect" worksheet

Optional – round pan of water

Procedures:

Ask the student what first comes to mind when they hear the word "attitude". Help the student define the word "attitude" as "how we think, affects how will feel, and how we act (what we say or do)". Point out that attitudes can be both negative or positive.

Ask the student if a situation like the following has ever happened to her: You go home in a good mood but mom (dad, brother, sister, grandma) comes home in a bad mood and soon everyone in the house is in a bad mood. Encourage the student to share.

Explain or demonstrate with the pan of water of how one drop of water in the middle creates a ripple that spreads throughout the entire pan of water, reaches the side of the pan, and then returns to the center. Relate that one drop of water to ourselves - our mood or attitude - and how our attitude can ripple out or affect others but can also return to us.

Discuss giving some positive and negative "what if attitude" scenarios such as:
 - *What if I got mad about a failing grade on my English paper and when Abby turned to speak to me I snapped at her to mind her own business. Abby in turn yelled at Whitney saying that she should bring her own pencil to school when Whitney asked if she could borrow a pencil. In turn, Whitney starting making fun of Missy for the way she talks and then Missy laughed at me when I dropped my papers and book off my desk.*

 - *What if I offered Abby an extra pencil when she forgot hers. In turn, Abby helped Whitney pick up her books that dropped from her desk. In turn, Whitney complimented Claire on her new pocketbook. In turn, Claire asked me to sit with them at lunch.*

Point out that we can only be in charge of our own attitudes – no one else's – therefore, we can focus on only starting positive ripples and when a negative ripple comes our way from someone else we do have the power to change the ripple from a negative to a positive. Discuss positive statements or ripples that can be used to counteract someone who says or does something that is not nice. What positive statements could you say if:
 ❊ Someone changes the TV channel without saying anything.
 ❊ Someone angrily pushes their books off their desk onto yours.
 ❊ Someone says, "Where did you get those awful looking shoes?"

Use the Ripple Effect worksheet to list their plan for starting positive ripples or to list a negative ripple from someone else and their plan to counteract the negative with positive. (In the circle at the center of the ripple write the first action, then write in the next circle write how the action affected the next person, and so on with the other outer circles.)

*adapted with permission from Sitsch and Senn (2002). Puzzle Pieces: The Classroom Guidance Connection. Chapin, SC: YouthLight, Inc.
www.youthlightbooks.com

RIPPLE EFFECT
W O R K S H E E T

Directions:
In the center of the ripple write either the negative or positive action. Then in the next outer circle write how the action affected another person, and in the next outer circle how it affected yet another person, and so forth. You may choose to practice your "what if" situations by writing a negative ripple received from someone else and how you can counteract the negative with a positive statement.

INDIVIDUAL COUNSELING ACTIVITIES

Your attitude affects others.
Send positive ripples.
Stop a negative ripple with
a caring comment.

Purpose:

To understand the possible reasons behind teasing/taunting and to be aware of ways to deal with the teasing/taunting.

Materials Needed:

Copy and cut out the "Teasing Wheel of Strategies on page 190. Assemble with a brad fastener.

Procedures:

Brainstorm together possible reasons why people tease others. Your list may include:

* When the teaser is insecure they may tease others to make themselves feel more superior.
* Trying to fit in or gain status with a group of friends.
* Some people may tease to get others to pay attention to them.
* Some tease to get back at others for something they think they did.
* Some teasers have grown up being teased by others and they think it is normal and accepted behavior.

Point out that by understanding the reason behind why a person teases it may help us to realize that their teasing could indicate a problem that the teaser may have rather than jumping to the conclusion that something is wrong with us or that the teaser is trying to be mean to us.

Brainstorm different strategies that can be used to deal with teasing/taunting. You may choose to refer to the "Teasing Wheel of Strategies" to review and discuss possible strategies to handle.

Put the strategies into action by encouraging the student to share teasing/taunting situations and then role-play effective strategies to handle.

INDIVIDUAL COUNSELING ACTIVITIES

TEASING WHEEL OF STRATEGIES
A C T I V I T Y   S H E E T *

Directions:
Copy and cut out the teasing strategy wheel and the arrow. Assemble with a fastening brad.

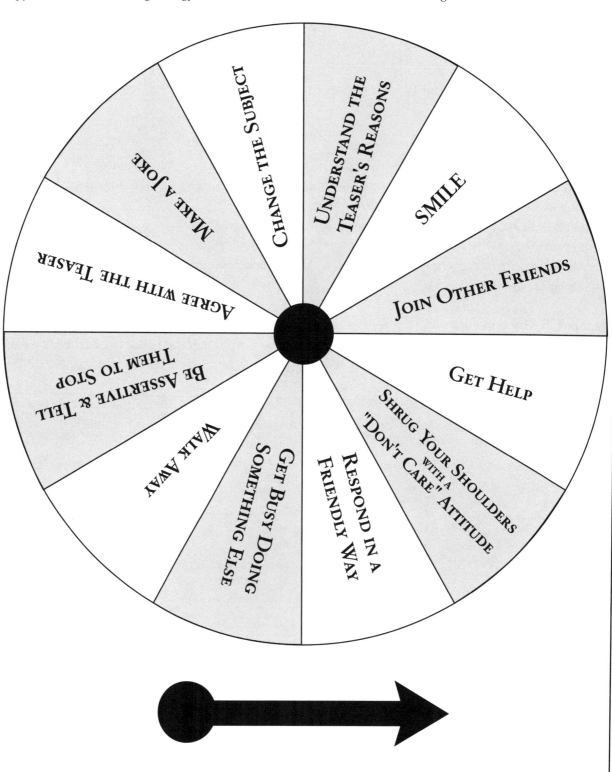

UNDERSTAND THE TEASER'S REASONS

SMILE

JOIN OTHER FRIENDS

GET HELP

SHRUG YOUR SHOULDERS WITH A "DON'T CARE" ATTITUDE

RESPOND IN A FRIENDLY WAY

GET BUSY DOING SOMETHING ELSE

WALK AWAY

BE ASSERTIVE & TELL THEM TO STOP

AGREE WITH THE TEASER

MAKE A JOKE

CHANGE THE SUBJECT

copied with permission from D. Senn (2006). Creative Approaches for Counseling Individual Children. Chapin, SC: YouthLight, Inc.
www.youthlightbooks.com

ACTIVITY 5

ANGER –
STAY under CONTROL

Purpose:

To focus on the feeling of anger and explore strategies to control and deal with the angry feeling.

Materials Needed:

Copy and cut apart the cards

Procedures:

Ask: *Have you ever said or done something when you were mad that you later regretted?* Discuss.

Explain that it's okay and normal to feel mad at times about something, but it is important to get control of the feelings so it doesn't do any damage.

Ask the student to share times that she has felt mad before. Ask: What have you found that helps you stay in control of your anger and is helpful? Explain the three rules of anger management:
1. You may not hurt yourself.
2. You may not hurt property.
3. You may not hurt others.

Review the strategies presented to see if they meet the criteria.

Share that you have cards of the DO's and DON'Ts of Anger Management but they are mixed up. Review the cards together, discussing and sorting in the correct stack.

DO'S AND DON'TS OF ANGER MANAGEMENT CARDS

Directions:
Copy and cut apart the cards. Review the cards together, discussing and sorting in the correct stack of a "do of anger management" and a "don't of anger management". On the blank cards, add your own thoughts for anger management.

Take deep breaths to calm down.	Revenge – get the person back.
Count backwards and tell yourself to chill.	Start a bad rumor about the person you're mad at.
Do something active, like exercise, to deal with the tension in the body.	Say something mean to the person and then add "Just kidding".
Sit down to help yourself calm down.	"Accidentally" bump into the person.
Write about it and then tear it up.	Decide never speak to the person again.
Talk about it with someone you trust.	With a mean look, yell a lot at the person.
Put it into perspective – there are worse things in life.	Blame others for the problem.
Get involved in an enjoyable activity to get your mind off the problem.	
Find humor in the situation.	
Forgive and move on.	

ACTIVITY 6

SAVE vs. DELETE

Purpose:

To emphasize the power a target of bullying behavior has in how she processes and chooses to let go of hurtful situations or events.

Materials Needed:

Access to a word processing program on the computer

Procedures:

As the student is sharing about her week and perhaps hurtful events in her week - reflect, summarize, and ask questions to clarify the events. If the student does not share anything good about her week, prompt with a question asking to recall a good event. If she is unable to recall a good event, create a good event with a compliment.

Refer to the computer and begin typing out her day / week with both the good and bad events.

Share that holding on to the negative or bad events and rethinking them in our head will not help us. Explain that we can re-write our day by deleting or sending to the trash the hurtful things that were said or done. Turn the computer over to the student and ask her to highlight and push the delete button or use the backspace to remove the hurtful information. Encourage the student that just as she deleted the hurtful parts of her day from her story on the computer she can delete or let go of the hurtful events in her life.

The student may choose to put the positive comments from her day in bold. Press the save button and then print a copy.

Remind the student that it is her choice of what to save or believe about what others say or do.

NEGATIVE THOUGHT SHREDDER

Purpose:
To help the target of bullying behavior by differentiating between negative and positive self-talk and to encourage the student to "get rid of" or "shred" the negative self talk.

Materials Needed:
Paper shredder

Copy and cut out the situations on the negative thought shredder situation sheet

Procedures:
Introduce the idea of self-talk. Explain that self-talk is the message we send to our brain about a situation – what we say to ourselves.

Ask the student to give examples of times that we have said positive things to ourselves that were helpful and then examples of negative things that we may say to ourselves that do not help.

Process how we feel with positive self-talk and with negative self-talk.

Explain that we need to get rid of negative self-talk. Introduce the paper shredder and explain how it "gets rid of" or shreds the paper. Relate the shredding of the paper to shredding or getting rid of the negative self-talks.

Read the first two examples of the situation on the activity sheet and ask the student to select and explain which is the positive self-talk and which is the negative self-talk – decide which to shred and which to keep. Next shred the negative self-talk slip of paper as you verbalize how you would get rid of the negative self-talk in your head. Read the positive self-talk and reinforce how that thought needs to stay with us.

Continue reading and shredding or saving the different thoughts about the situations on the activity sheet.

Then ask the student to write down a situation she might be dealing with and create both negative and positive self-talk. Then go through the process of shredding the negative and saving the positive.

Encourage/challenge the student to focus on the positive self-talk in future problem situations.

NEGATIVE THOUGHT SHREDDER SITUATIONS

Directions:

For each situation, ask the student to select and explain which is the positive self-talk and which is the negative self-talk. Then shred the negative self-talk slip of paper using the paper shredder. As you do this, verbalize how you would get rid of the negative self-talk in your head. Read the positive self-talk and reinforce how that thought needs to stay with you. Create situations of your own on the blank situation slips.

1a. **PROBLEM SITUATION:** Being teased about a "bad hair day".

SELF-TALK: "Oh, I know my hair does look horrible. I'm just not pretty or popular."

1b. **PROBLEM SITUATION:** Being teased about a "bad hair day".

SELF-TALK: "Hey, it's only hair. I'm not going to let their rudeness bother me. I've got to go work on that science project."

2a. **PROBLEM SITUATION:** Not getting invited to a friend's party.

SELF-TALK: "Why didn't I get invited? Does she not like me. I guess I don't really have any friends. No one likes me."

2b. **PROBLEM SITUATION:** Not getting invited to a friend's party.

SELF-TALK: "Looks like I did get left out. I need to find me something else to do Friday night. I think I'll call my friend from church to see if she wants to come over Friday."

3a. **PROBLEM SITUATION:** All my close friends ended up with a different lunch break, I don't have any close friends to sit with at lunch.

SELF-TALK: "This is terrible, I can't even go into the lunch room, everyone will stare and think that I'm a loser."

3b. **PROBLEM SITUATION:** All my close friends ended up with a different lunch break, I don't have any close friends to sit with at lunch.

SELF-TALK: "It is a little scary going into the lunch room when I don't know where or who I'll sit with, but I will just have to smile and look for someone I know and see if I can join them and get to know them better."

4a. **PROBLEM SITUATION:** Shannon just told me that there is a rumor going around about me liking some guy. I don't even know the guy.

SELF-TALK: "I bet it was Kelsey who started that rumor. Just wait 'til I see her – I'll get back at her for talking about me."

4b. **PROBLEM SITUATION:** Shannon just told me that there is a rumor going around about me liking some guy. I don't even know the guy.

SELF-TALK: "Boy that is funny, the word is I like some guy I've never met. Wouldn't it turn out funny if we did meet and we did like each other!"

5a. **PROBLEM SITUATION:** _____

_____

SELF-TALK: _____

_____

5b. **PROBLEM SITUATION:** _____

_____

SELF-TALK: _____

_____

Purpose:

To encourage the target of bullying behavior to refocus on the clearer picture of what may be behind the bully situation.

Materials Needed:

Binoculars, if available

Procedures:

Ask the student if she has ever looked through binoculars when they were not focused yet. Ask them to explain what the "picture" looked like and what they had to do to "clear up" the picture. If you have binoculars available, take time to look through with it first out of focus and then clearing up the picture.

Relate a bullying situation (use an example the student can relate to such as: exclusion, teasing/taunting, controlling, etc.) to the out of focus picture through the binoculars. That perhaps our first look at a situation doesn't always give us a clear or correct picture of the situation. We might first think that something is wrong with us, that we are a bad person or an unworthy person as to why someone else doesn't seem to accept or like us. Discuss reasons behind bullying behavior such as to show off, for power, or to go along or "fit in" with a group. Explain that when we understand the behavior behind the bullying we can see the picture more clearly and not take the "attack" as personal.

You may choose to role-play different bullying situations. Encourage the student to share personal stories that can be processed using the binocular analogy.

INDIVIDUAL COUNSELING ACTIVITIES

REFRAMING*

Purpose:

To help targets of bullying behavior reframe the difficult situation in a positive way.

Materials Needed:

Copy on heavy paper and cut out the picture frames on page 199 of the Frame It! Activity Sheet.

Copy and cut out the picture situations on the Frame It! Activity Sheet.

Blank paper, pencils/markers

Procedures:

Discuss the purpose of a frame for a picture – to add decoration to the picture.

Display the two picture frames (the positive thought frame and the negative thought frame) and review the messages of each frame. Relate that how we choose to look at a situation – the frame we put on it – can help the situation or make it worse.

Review/discuss the situation pictures first putting the negative frame and discussing the typical negative thoughts a person may have about the situation and then switching the situation to the positive frame and discussing positive thoughts a person could have about the situation. Review for practice any or all of the situations given.

Next give a blank piece of paper that the student can draw a picture of one of their own problem situations that needs reframing. Process using the frames.

*adapted with permission from D. Senn (2003) Small Group Counseling for Children (Grades 2-5). Chapin, SC. YouthLight, Inc.
www.youthlightbooks.com

FRAME IT! ACTIVITY SHEET

Directions:

Copy on heavy paper and cut out the two picture frames – don't forget to cut out the center of the frames. Copy and cut out the four picture situations on the following page. Practice reframing the difficult situation with the positive frame. Review what you would be thinking or saying to your self.

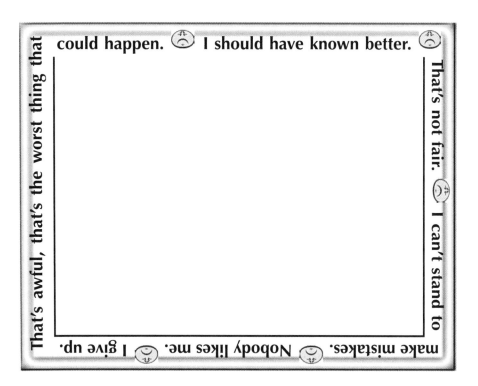

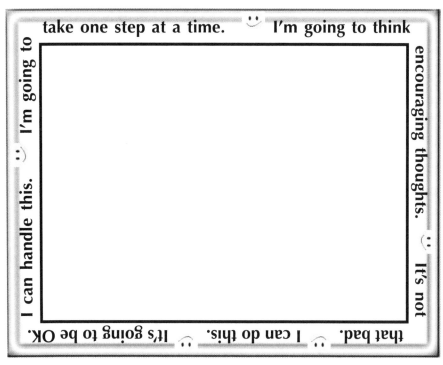

INDIVIDUAL COUNSELING ACTIVITIES

"You got the 'cold shoulder' when you tried to sit with a friend at lunch."

"You didn't get invited to the party."

"You feel like others are talking about you."

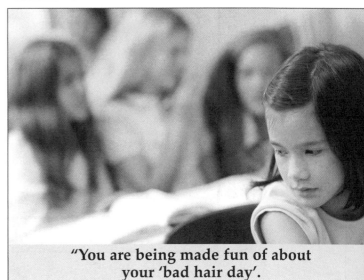

"You are being made fun of about your 'bad hair day'."

MATCHING UP "QUICK FIXES" TO THE BULLYING PROBLEM

Purpose:

To provide various strategies and "Quick Fixes" for the target of bullying behavior to utilize and deal with different types of bullying situations.

Materials Needed:

Copy and cut apart the Fast Fix Cards Worksheet

Procedures:

Review examples of ways that girls can be mean to other girls. As you talk, place each of the MEAN BEHAVIOR CARDS spread out on a table. Encourage the student to talk and share, giving examples about each of the behaviors.

Next hand the student a stack of QUICK FIX CARDS. Instruct the student to place each QUICK FIX CARD underneath a MEAN BEHAVIOR CARD. (Some of the "Quick Fix" cards can be used for several mean behaviors. The student can just choose where they think it best fits.)

Review and discuss.

Allow the student to either put the QUICK FIX CARDS in an envelop or bag to take with her or select a MEAN BEHAVIOR CARD and turn it over and copy down the "quick fixes" that could be used to help the situation.

QUICK FIX CARDS WORKSHEET

MEAN BEHAVIOR CARD:
She rolls her eyes
and acts as if she
is better than I am.

MEAN BEHAVIOR CARD:
I feel like if I don't do what
she says she will talk bad
about me and turn my
friends against me.

MEAN BEHAVIOR CARD:
She doesn't invite
or include me in the group's
activities anymore.

MEAN BEHAVIOR CARD:
She is always
accidentally/on purpose
bumping into me
in the hall.

MEAN BEHAVIOR CARD:
She says I can trust her
but she keeps telling
others what I asked her
to keep private.

FAST FIX CARD:
Don't give the power
to the other person – you
don't have to believe
what they said.

MEAN BEHAVIOR CARD:
She is always saying something mean and then adds,
"Just kidding." It doesn't
feel like she's 'just kidding'.

FAST FIX CARD:
Review your positive
qualities and be
proud of who you are.

FAST FIX CARD:
Resist the temptation to
"get back" at the person –
don't stoop to their level.

FAST FIX CARD:
Ask the person to stop.

FAST FIX CARD:
Let your real friends
know it's not true.

FAST FIX CARD:
Walk away.

FAST FIX CARD:
Laugh it off.

FAST FIX CARD:
Don't take it personally,
realize it may have resulted
from someone's need for
power or control.

FAST FIX CARD:
Label it as a
ridiculous
rumor.

FAST FIX CARD:
Hold your head
high and appreciate
your good values.

FAST FIX CARD:
Use your
anger control.

FAST FIX CARD:
Ignore,
look bored.

FAST FIX CARD:
Remember that the
hurt will heal.

FAST FIX CARD:
Assertively confront
the friend.

FAST FIX CARD:
Forgive, forget, and move on.
Holding resentment and
anger is not worth it.

FAST FIX CARD:
Rebuild your ability
to trust – not everyone
will mistreat the trust.

BULLY PROOF SHIELD in ACTION

Purpose:

To provide five strategies for handling the situation when you are a target of bullying.

Materials Needed:

Poster board paper and markers to create a large Bully Proof Defense Shield and several sheets of paper that can be crumpled into a ball to represent bullying behavior.

Procedures:

The "Bully Proof Defense Shield" was shared in Lesson 3 of the Classroom Guidance section. The creation of the shield can be used as a follow up in individual counseling. The individual counseling session allows time to personalize the use of the shield to real life bullying situations she is facing and to role-play the shield's use to help.

Ask the student about her week, listening and responding. As bullying incidents are shared – exclusion, target of gossip or rumors, bossing, controlling, manipulating, taunting, behind your back, physical threats, pushing, shoving, better than you behavior, or intimidations – make a note of these behaviors to use as a role play later in the session.

Show the "Bully Proof Defense Shield" on page _____ and relate how a shield can be used as protection against harm. Explain that a common form of girl bullying is relational aggression and includes more of the indirect bullying - the defense shield isn't designed to physically protect from bullying but the information on the shield can provide a way of positive thinking that can protect us from the more covert or indirect bullying.

From the poster board sheet, cut out and create a personalized Bully Proof Defense Shield.
In section one: Copy the sentence about "Just because someone called me a name or said something mean doesn't make it true."
In section two: Add the sentence "I will believe in myself. I am not defined by others." Ask the student to write what she is good at, a good quality, and something she has done recently that she is proud of.
In section three: Explain the idea of self-talk and ask the student to create a positive self-talk to counteract a bullying behavior and write it in a thought bubble.
In section four: Brainstorm together okay things to say or do to handle a bully situation well. Direct the student to add these to the fourth section of the shield.
In section five: Ask the student to write, "If appropriate – report it."

Next, refer to the list of bullying situations she has experienced. Crumple several sheets of paper into balls. Gently throw a ball of paper toward the student explaining that the ball of paper represents a bully behavior she has experienced. The student needs to hold the shield up for protection against the ball of paper. Process how the shield protects her but to do so she had to make the effort to use the shield – relate this to the importance of making the effort to use the various positive thoughts and actions to deal with bullying behavior effectively.

BULLY PROOF DEFENSE SHIELD

1.

Just because someone called me a name or said something mean, doesn't make it true.

☐ TRUE   ☐ FALSE

2.

I will believe in myself. Who I am is not defined by others.

Right Turn Only →

Head in the "right" direction.

I am good at ⎯ ⎯ ⎯ ⎯ ⎯ ⎯

One of my good qualities is ⎯ ⎯ ⎯ ⎯

Recently, I am proud that I ⎯ ⎯ ⎯ ⎯

3. What positive self-talk is in your thought bubble?

4. **Okay things to "DO"**

_____

_____

and "SAY"

_____

_____

Bullying is NOT OKAY

_____

Purpose:

To provide a framework for the problem-solving process

Materials Needed:

Copy of the Problem Solving Model Worksheet

Pencil/pen

Procedures:

In working with students individually in reviewing a problem seeking to form a plan to manage or resolve, it is helpful to share with the student the framework or questions to lead the student through the process. By giving the student this outline of questions and helping the student to know how to use it then the student can use this same process with future problems.

Share the Problem Solving Model Worksheet with the student. Read and discuss each question allowing time for the student to write down the answers to form her plan.

PROBLEM-SOLVING MODEL
W O R K S H E E T

1. What is the problem? _____

_____.

2. What have you tried? _____

_____.

3. What else could you do? List the possibilities. For each of the possibilities you just listed, think about and write a possible positive outcome and a negative outcome of each.

POSSIBILITY #1: _____

*Positive outcome:*_____

Negative outcome: _____

POSSIBILITY #2: _____

*Positive outcome:*_____

Negative outcome: _____

POSSIBILITY #3: _____

*Positive outcome:*_____

Negative outcome: _____

POSSIBILITY #4: _____

*Positive outcome:*_____

Negative outcome: _____

4. From the possibilities and outcomes listed in step 3, which do you want to try first?

_____

5. What is your plan of how to implement. Include the when, the where, the how.

_____

_____

If the first possibility isn't successful, try a different possibility.

WHAT ARE YOU WORTH?

𝒫urpose:

To acknowledge both our admirable qualities and our fake, hurtful qualities by using the analogy of a diamond and cubic zirconia. Focus is on strengthening our admirable qualities.

𝓜aterials 𝒩eeded:

Picture of or example of a diamond and a cubic zirconia, if possible

Copy of the "How Will You Shine?" Worksheet

Pencil/pen

𝒫rocedures:

Ask: *What comes to mind when you think of a diamond?* Share some about the history of a diamond: begins as a rough diamond that is mined and then heat and high pressure are added to clean the diamond, next a skilled laborer cuts the diamond into it's present shape.

Point out how we can compare ourselves to a diamond:
both are valuable on the inside from the beginning
after work and effort we can let ourselves/the diamond shine clear and strong (Our admirable qualities will shine and sparkle)

Point out that a cubic zirconia can also shine and sparkle but that it doesn't have the same value as a diamond and is man-made. There may be times that we or others want to take short cuts, perhaps through manipulation or control, in order to be popular and shine. This type of sparkle and shine is "fake" and doesn't have the lasting ability of the diamond's sparkle and shine.

Ask the student to complete the worksheet – "How Will You Shine?" as she considers how to achieve the TRUE shine and sparkle in her life.

HOW WILL YOU SHINE?
W O R K S H E E T

Directions:

Answer the following questions as you consider how to achieve the TRUE shine and sparkle in your life.

✳ **List your admirable qualities that allow you to truly shine.**

_____

_____

_____

_____

✳ **List the fake qualities that you may be tempted to use as a short cut to gain power and shine.**

_____

_____

_____

_____

✳ **What is your plan to shine clear and strong in a good way?**

_____

_____

_____

_____

_____

INDIVIDUAL COUNSELING ACTIVITIES

ACTIVITY 14	BEHAVIOR CHANGE NEEDED

Purpose:
To acknowledge inappropriate behavior and to make a plan for a change of behavior.

Materials Needed:
Copy of the Behavior Change Worksheet on page 93.

Pencil/pen

Procedures:
(If your individual counseling student participated in Class Lesson 2: What's in Your Heart? reference this lesson as you talk with the student)

Tell the student to pretend that we are fast forwarding to 10 years in the future.
Ask: *How do you think people would describe what kind of person you are?*

Ask: *How would someone describe the kind of person you are now?*

If there is a discrepancy between how they would like to be described in the future and how they would be described now due to some inappropriate behaviors, offer to help the student target a specific behavior and develop a plan for improvement.

(If the student sees no inappropriate behavior, however you are aware of poor behavior choices, you may choose to ask their teacher and perhaps some of their peers about how they would describe the student. Gain the student's permission to do this. If after gathering information and there is a discrepancy between how the student sees her behavior and how other's see her behavior then use your counseling skills to gently confront with this information seeking to help the student recognize and agree that a behavior change would be helpful.)

Ask the student to pinpoint a specific behavior that she would choose to work on for improvement to become the kind of person she wants to be.

Share a copy of the Behavior Change Worksheet on page 93. Work together through each step in order to create a plan for change.

ACTIVITY 15

EMPATHY BUILDING

Purpose:
To understand and practice empathy

Materials Needed:
Copy of the Feeling Vocabulary List and the "I Care" Plan

Pencil/pen

Procedures:
Ask: *What does empathy mean?* Explain that empathy is the ability to identify with someone else's thoughts and feelings and what they are experiencing. Ask: Why do you think it is important to have empathy for others?

Explain that in order to have empathy for others we need to understand what a person may be thinking or feeling in a situation. Invite the student to practice some of the following what if situations. Review with the student the Feeling Vocabulary list (fold the sheet in half with the feeling vocabulary list showing) to help in identifying the feelings in the following situations:

* How would you feel if people made fun of you because your family didn't have money to buy "fashionable" clothes?
* How would you feel if a close friend told one of your secrets?
* How would you feel if you were left out when your group of friends went to the movies together?
* How would you feel if you were the new girl at school?
* How would you feel when your best friend won't talk to you anymore because of an untrue rumor about you liking the same guy that she likes.

Ask: *What does the saying "reach out and help someone" mean? What are some ways that we can help others? How does empathy play a role in this?*

Encourage the student to think about the people she comes in contact with – at school, in the neighborhood, and at home. Ask the student to select one person this week who she is aware of that she can empathize with and that could use her help. Discuss the situation she has chosen and create a plan to help - include the why, what, how, when, and where. Complete the "I Care" Plan on the bottom half of the folded sheet. Encourage the student to take the sheet with them as a reference in thinking of other's feelings and as a reminder of the her plan.

FEELING VOCABULARY LIST

Empathy is the ability to understand another person's thoughts and feelings and what they are experiencing. The following is a list of feeling words that may help us more accurately identify and relate to someone else's feelings in a situation.

disappointed	angry	exhausted	anxious
frustrated	furious	hurt	shy
worried	calm	bored	lonely
confused	excited	nervous	guilty
humiliated	content	happy	confident
embarrassed	distracted	miserable	self-conscious

THE "I CARE" PLAN

I CARE...

WHY _____

WHAT is the situation _____

HOW do I think I can be of help

_____

_____

_____

WHEN and WHERE can I help

_____

_____

_____

INDIVIDUAL COUNSELING ACTIVITIES

HEARTPRINTS*

Purpose:

To encourage the sharing of kind and caring deeds – leaving heartprints behind.

Materials Needed:

Cut out heart and pen/marker

Procedures:

Ask the student what comes to mind when they think of a valentine heart – what does it represent or symbolize? Focus on the answers of kindness and caring. Next, ask the student to explain what a footprint is – respond as a print that is left behind by a foot. Then ask them to guess what a "heartprint" might be. Summarize a "heartprint" as "sharing your kindness and care with others – leaving the print of your heart behind".

Ask the student to share ways that other people have shared their kindness and care about you.

Ask the student to share ways she could show kindness and care for others this week – ways to leave her heartprints behind.

Write the assignment or plan on a cut out heart to take as a reminder.

INDIVIDUAL COUNSELING ACTIVITIES

*Heartprint concept from the children's book entitled Heartprints by P.K.Halliman (1999). Ideals Children's Books: Nashville, Tennessee.

References

Beane, A., (1999). *The Bully Free Classroom*. Minneapolis, MN: Free Spirit Publishing Inc.

Bolton, J. and Graeve, S., (2005). *No Room for Bullies*. Boys Town, Nebraska: Boys Town Press.

Bowen, A. and Randall, K., *Mean Girls* Professional Seminar, Chapin, SC: Developmental Resources, Inc.

Coloroso, B., (2003). *The Bully, the Bullied, and the Bystander*. New York, NY: HarperCollins Publisher Inc.

Crick, N.R. and Grutpeter, J.K. (1995). "Relational Aggression, Gender, and Social Psychological Adjustment." *Child Development*, 66, 710-722

Criswell, P., (2003). *A Smart Girl's Guide to Friendship Troubles*. Middleton, WI: Pleasant Company Publications.

Dellasega, C. and Nixon, C., (2003). *Girl Wars*. NewYork, NY: Simon and Schuster, Inc.

Fried S. and Fried P., (1994). *Bullies and Victims*. New York, NY: M. Evans and Company

Hallinan P.K., (2002). *Heartprints*. Nashville, Tennessee: Ideals Children's Books of Ideals Publication and division of Guideposts.

Ludwig, T., (2005). *My Secret Bully*. Berkeley, Toronto: Tricycle Press.

National Association of School Psychologists (NASP)

Senn, D. (2006). *Creative Approaches for Counseling Individual Children*. Chapin, SC: YouthLight, Inc.

Senn, D. (2003). *Small Group Counseling for Children (Grades 2-5)*. Chapin, SC: YouthLight, Inc.

Sitsch, G. and Senn, D., (2002). *Puzzle Pieces...Classroom Guidance Connection*. Chapin, SC: YouthLight, Inc.